The Mycophile's Handbook

From Spores to Harvest: Your Comprehensive Guide to Mushroom

Jackson Reynolds

Table of Contents

INTRODUCTION

"The Mycophile's Handbook: From Spores to Harvest: Your Comprehensive Guide to Mushroom" takes readers on a fascinating trip through the intriguing field of mycology. Exploring the complex world of mushrooms, this book is a must-have resource for both new growers and experienced mycologists.

Join us as we explore the wonders of mushrooms, from their modest spores to the abundant harvests they produce. It's going to be an exciting journey. We carefully review all of the necessary instruments and methods for productive growth, from choosing the suitable substrate to creating ideal fruiting environments.

Beyond the useful features, this handbook offers a wide range of mushroom species profiles that provide details on their distinct qualities, cultivation needs, and culinary delights. Every type of mushroom, from the well-known button mushroom to the mysterious truffle, is carefully studied and comes with delicious recipes and dietary advice.

Going a step further, we examine the skill of foraging for wild mushrooms, covering the sustainable methods, identification methods, and safety measures necessary for a successful hunt. Furthermore, we reveal the complex ecological and therapeutic functions of fungi, illuminating their mycorrhizal connections, mycoremediation capacities, and medicinal advantages.

Whether you're interested in mycology cooking or are just fascinated by the wonders of nature, "The Mycophile's Handbook" is the best resource for learning about mushrooms and developing tremendous respect for these amazing creatures.

CHAPTER I

Getting Started

The Fascinating World of Fungi

Despite being a vast kingdom of organisms, fungi are essential to ecosystems worldwide, but they are frequently overlooked and remain unexplained. Fungi come in a stunning variety of shapes and sizes, from the enormous mushrooms seen on the forest floor to the tiny molds that grow in our homes. We explore the biology, ecological significance, cultural value, and prospective uses in numerous disciplines of fungi in this section, delving into the fascinating world of fungi.

The fundamental aspect of fungal biology is their distinct feeding strategy. Fungi are heterotrophic animals that get their nutrients by absorbing organic matter from their surroundings, in contrast to plants, which make their food through photosynthesis. Fungi secrete enzymes that disassemble complex organic molecules into simpler ones, and these chemicals can be absorbed and used by the fungi for growth and reproduction. Because of their saprotrophic nature, fungi are vital decomposers in ecosystems, helping to produce soil and cycle nutrients. Mushrooms are among the most famous and identifiable types of fungi. Many fungi use these fruiting bodies as their reproductive structures. They arise from the mycelium, the subterranean fungal hyphae network. The shapes, sizes, and colors of mushrooms are astounding; they range from the standard button mushrooms available in supermarkets to the exotic and transient varieties that flourish in far-off rainforests. In addition to being delicious, mushrooms have a rich cultural history and are frequently used in traditional Chinese medicine, art, and folklore worldwide.

But mushrooms only make up a small portion of the diversity of fungi. Molds, yeasts, lichens, and many more types of creatures are included in the fungal kingdom. For example, molds are commonplace fungi that grow in various environments, such as moist basements and decomposing organic materials. While many molds are advantageous—such as those used to make cheese, soy sauce, and antibiotics—other molds can harm structures and cause food to decay, endangering the health of both people and animals.

On the other hand, single-celled fungi called yeasts are well-known for their function in fermentation. Through a process known as anaerobic respiration, these microscopic organisms transform sugars into alcohol and carbon dioxide. Humans have used this process for millennia to create alcoholic beverages like wine, beer, and bread. Additionally, yeasts are used as model organisms in scientific studies, which advances our knowledge of metabolism, cell biology, and genetics.

Another fantastic example of a fungal symbiotic relationship is lichens. Lichens comprise a fungus, usually from the phylum Ascomycota or Basidiomycota, and algae or cyanobacteria, which are partners in photosynthetic processes. Because of their symbiotic relationship, lichens may thrive in harsh settings, including cliffs, deserts, and Arctic tundra. These areas serve crucial ecological roles as pioneer species and soil stabilizers. In addition to stimulating artistic and scientific curiosity, lichens have been used as sources of natural pigments and dyes as well as environmental quality indicators.

Fungi are essential to ecology and culture, but they can also be used in a wide range of industries, such as biotechnology, agriculture, medicine, and bioremediation. Numerous bioactive substances with medicinal qualities, such as immunosuppressants, antibiotics, and anticancer drugs, are produced by fungi. For instance, the 20th century saw a revolution in medicine with the discovery of penicillin, an antibiotic derived from the fungus Penicillium that saved many lives and helped pave the way for the creation of other antimicrobial medications.

Fungi are important in agriculture because they are pathogens, decomposers, and plant symbionts. Most land plants' roots create mutualistic relationships with mycorrhizal fungi, improving nutrient intake and fostering resilient, growing plants. On the other side, plant-pathogenic fungi can cause devastating illnesses in crops, resulting in significant losses in terms of quality and yield. By comprehending the intricate relationships that exist between fungi and plants, scientists can create tactics for sustainable farming, such as utilizing biocontrol agents and improving soil health.

Fungi also hold promise for environmental cleansing and restoration in the field of bioremediation. By enzymatic activities, some fungi can break down a variety of contaminants, such as pesticides, heavy metals, and hydrocarbons. This fungus, referred to as bioremediation, can be applied to clean up polluted soil and water, offering affordable and long-lasting solutions to environmental problems. Fungi are also being investigated for their potential in biomass conversion, waste management, and the generation of renewable energy, underscoring their adaptability and promise as bioresources.

Fungi are essential suppliers of proteins, secondary metabolites, and enzymes in biotechnology that are used in many different sectors. Because of their capacity to catalyze biochemical reactions, fungus-derived enzymes, including cellulases, amylases, and proteases, find extensive application in the food, textile, and detergent industries. In addition, fungi generate specialty enzymes with desirable characteristics like thermostability and specificity, making them useful in biocatalysis and bioprocessing. Moreover, the growth of a bio-based economy is aided by the engineering of fungi to produce biofuels, bioplastics, and other sustainable materials.

In conclusion, a wide range of creatures with distinct biological adaptations and ecological roles can be found in fungi's complex and intriguing world. Fungi, from the enormous mushrooms on the forest floor to the little molds in our homes, are an essential and expected part of ecosystems all around the world. Fungi have immense potential for use in biotechnology, bioremediation, medicine, and agriculture, in addition to their ecological relevance. These applications could address urgent issues with food security, human health, and environmental sustainability, among other things. We better understand the complex web of life on Earth and our connection to the natural world as we continue to solve the mysteries surrounding fungi and utilize their potential.

Tools and Equipment You'll Need

Having the appropriate tools and equipment can make all the difference in an endeavor's success or failure. A well-stocked toolkit is crucial for starting a professional job, a DIY project, or a new pastime. This section examines the wide variety of tools and equipment required for different jobs, ranging from woodworking and home repairs to gardening and culinary endeavors.

A basic toolset is essential for duties related to house maintenance and repairs. Essential hand tools, including screwdrivers, wrenches, pliers, hammers, and tape measures, are usually included in this toolbox. Screwdrivers are tools used for driving or extracting screws. They are available in many sizes and styles, such as flathead and Phillips head. Pliers are multipurpose instruments for grasping, bending, and cutting wires, whereas wrenches are used to tighten or loosen nuts and bolts. While tape measures offer precise measurements for cutting materials or figuring out dimensions, hammers are necessary for pounding nails or tapping objects into position.

Power tools are essential for construction and home repair projects in addition to manual equipment. With the right accessories, power drills are multipurpose instruments that can be used for driving screws, stirring paint, and drilling holes; for fast and accurate cutting of plastic, metal, or wood, circular saws, and jigsaws are necessary. While routers are essential for cutting edges and making artistic patterns, sanders are used for smoothing uneven surfaces and removing paint and varnish. When utilizing power tools, safety gear, including goggles, gloves, and ear protection is crucial to preventing mishaps and injuries.

The fulfilling pastime of woodworking calls for specific tools and equipment to shape, join, and finish wood. Hand tools for shaping and cutting wood by hand, such as chisels, planes, saws, and clamps, are usually included in a woodworking toolbox. While planes are necessary for smoothing surfaces and eliminating flaws, chisels are used for carving or sculpting wood. Several hand saws are available for accurately and precisely cutting wood, such as dovetail, rip, and crosscut saws. For securely keeping wood components together during assembly or glue-up, clamps are essential.

Power tools are necessary in addition to hand tools for more accurate and efficient woodworking. The two main cutting instruments for accurately and quickly ripping, crosscutting, and mitering wood are table saws and miter saws. A band saw or scroll saw is a valuable tool for cutting curves, complex shapes, and patterns in wood and other materials. Woodworking routers are needed for cutting joints, shaping edges, and adding decorative features. Before finishing, sanders are used to smooth surfaces and remove defects; wood lathes are essential for turning symmetrical or cylindrical objects like spindles, bowls, and pens.

The correct tools and equipment are needed for planting, growing, and maintaining plants and landscapes in gardening, which is a fulfilling hobby. Hand tools for digging, planting, and weeding, such as trowels, pruners, shovels, and rakes, are usually included in an essential gardening toolkit. Pruners are used to shape and trim plants, while trowels are used for small-hole gardening, seedling transplanting, and soil loosening. Shovels are available in different varieties, such as digging shovels, scoops, and spades, which are used for moving mulch, soil, and other materials. Rakes are essential for mulching lawns and gardens, leveling the soil, and clearing waste. Power tools and equipment and hand tools can help increase productivity and simplify gardening chores. String trimmers are used for trimming edges and removing grass and weeds in hard-to-reach places, while lawn mowers are necessary for keeping a clean and well-manicured lawn. For cutting and shaping hedges, shrubs, and bushes, hedge trimmers are needed; leaf blowers and vacuums are necessary for removing leaves and other debris from lawns, driveways, and sidewalks. Hoses, sprinklers, and drip lines are examples of irrigation systems necessary for effectively watering plants and landscapes while preserving water.

The proper tools and equipment are essential for precise and elegant food preparation, cooking, and serving in culinary endeavors. Necessary kitchen utensils include pots and pans, knives, cutting boards, and other items for chopping, slicing, sautéing, and boiling food. Cutting boards offer a sturdy surface for chopping and slicing, while knives are essential for various culinary operations like dicing, mincing, and carving. For boiling, frying, braising, and baking, pots and pans are available in a variety of sizes and materials, such as cast iron, nonstick, and stainless steel.

Specialized equipment can improve culinary creativity and efficiency in addition to standard kitchen instruments. While blenders and immersion blenders are necessary for creating smoothies, soups, sauces, and purees, stand mixers and food processors are indispensable for effortlessly mixing, blending, and cutting items. For correct measurement of ingredients and recipe execution, kitchen scales and measuring cups are essential, while thermometers guarantee exact cooking temperatures for meats, candies, and baked products. Pasta makers, bread makers, and sous vide immersion circulators are examples of specialty equipment that may take home cooking to a new level by facilitating experimentation and the discovery of new flavors and methods.

To sum up, having the proper tools and equipment is crucial for success and enjoyment in various jobs and endeavors, from carpentry and house repairs to gardening and culinary activities. A well-stocked toolkit allows people to approach problems with courage and imagination, meaningfully and fulfillingly expressing their skills and passions. Individuals may reap the advantages of practical performance, accurate outcomes, and long-lasting durability by purchasing high-quality instruments and taking good care of them. This way, they can be adequately equipped for all the duties and adventures that lie ahead.

Understanding Mushroom Anatomy

Mushrooms arouse our curiosity and engage our senses with their various forms, sizes, and colors. These mysterious creatures are members of the kingdom Fungi and are essential to ecosystems all across the planet. Comprehending the structure of mushrooms is crucial for recognizing edible varieties, enjoying their aesthetic value, and understanding their ecological role. This section delves into mushrooms' anatomy, physiology, and environmental roles, examining their complex structures from the top of their crowns to the depths of their mycelial networks.

The most noticeable aspect of the mushroom above ground is its fruiting body, which comprises a stem, cap, and occasionally pores or gills beneath. Diverse species, called pileus, have diverse forms, textures, and colors for their caps. While some mushrooms have flat, umbonate, or vase-shaped caps, others have convex caps. The cap's surface may be wart-covered, scaly, wrinkled, or smooth, depending on the species. The cap can be white, yellow, brown, red, or even blue, and it frequently has distinct patterns or gradients that help identify the species. Behind the cap, the stem, or the stipe, offers support and attaches the cap to the substrate. There are differences in the stems' length, thickness, and texture; some mushrooms have thin, long stems, while others have short, robust ones. The stem's surface might be fibrous, smooth, or decorated with scales, rings, or pieces of the global veil, which is a membrane that surrounds the developing fruiting body and acts as protection. Though they may range in tone or saturation, the color of the stem and cap frequently match.

Numerous mushrooms are distinguished primarily by their reproductive structures, which are situated on the underside of the cap. These structures, which are thin, blade-like plates that radiate from the stem toward the cap's edge, are called lamellae or gills. Millions of minute spores are produced and dispersed by the gills, where they are discharged into the atmosphere upon maturity. Different mushrooms have different gill arrangements and attachments; some have free gills that are not in contact with the stem, while others have connected or decurrent gills that extend the entire stem length.

Certain mushrooms include pores, tiny holes on the underside of the cap through which spores are discharged, and gills. Included in the Boletales order are pore-bearing mushrooms, which include well-known edible species like chanterelles (Cantharellus spp.) and porcini (Boletus edulis). Different species of mushrooms have different pore sizes, shapes, and colors. For example, some species have big, angular pores, while others have tiny, spherical pores. Pore-bearing mushrooms usually have a central stalk or a bulbous base instead of a distinct stem.

Although mushrooms' exterior characteristics are easily observed, their inside structures are just as fascinating and crucial to comprehending their biology and ecology. Mushrooms are microscopic organisms made up of specialized cells arranged into tissues and organs that have different purposes. The cuticle, which is the mushroom's outermost covering, acts as a barrier to protect the surface of the stem and cap. Specialized cells known as cystidia, which are involved in defense, moisture management, and spore distribution, may be present in the cuticle.

The reproductive structures necessary for spore formation are located beneath the cuticle in the mushroom's flesh or hymenium. The hymenium of gilled mushrooms is found on the gill surface and is made up of basidia, which are closely spaced cells with spores on their surfaces. Nuclear division and meiosis typically result in the production of four spores per basidium, giving rise to genetically varied progeny. The hymenium of pore-bearing mushrooms comprises tubes lined with basidia that discharge spores into the confined space. The hymenium is found on the surface of the pores.

The fungal body of the mushroom is made up of a web of hyphae, which are slender filaments that resemble threads. In order to create a complex network known as the mycelium, hyphae elongate at the terminals and branch widely. The mycelium then spreads throughout the substrate and uses enzymatic digestion to collect nutrients. The fungal mycelium, which is its vegetative portion, is essential to the decomposition process, cycling of nutrients, and symbiotic relationships with other organisms. Mycelial networks are highly linked and can cover enormous tracts of soil, wood, or other substrates.

Apart from their vegetative and reproductive structures, mushrooms have adaptations that improve their ability to survive and procreate in various settings. Certain mushrooms release poisons or bitter substances to discourage herbivores and lessen competition with other creatures. Others create volatile organic compounds

(VOCs) that draw animals or insects and aid in the spread of spores. Certain mushrooms associate mutualistically with bacteria, plants, or algae, trading resources and nutrients in symbiotic relationships. These modifications let mushrooms thrive ecologically and remain resilient in various global settings.

In conclusion, comprehending the anatomy of mushrooms is crucial to appreciating their diversity, beauty, and ecological significance. A surprising variety of structures and adaptations that represent their environmental responsibilities and evolutionary history can be seen in mushrooms, ranging from the exquisite patterns of their caps to the complicated networks of their mycelia. by studying muscle analysis, scientists and enthusiasts can deepen their understanding of fungi and their impact on ecosystems, human health, and cultural heritage. Mushrooms continue to arouse amazement and curiosity in people of all ages and backgrounds, whether they are collected for their culinary worth, studied for their scientific relevance, or appreciated for their aesthetic appeal.

CHAPTER II

Cultivating Mushrooms

Choosing the Right Species for Your Environment

The success and sustainability of any endeavor, whether gardening, landscaping, or habitat restoration, depend heavily on the species you choose for your area. The species you select should be compatible with the particulars of your location, such as the soil type, climate, amount of sunlight, and water availability. By carefully weighing these criteria and choosing species that are suited to flourish in your particular ecosystem, you can establish a resilient and biodiverse habitat that benefits both local wildlife and human activity.

Evaluating your area's temperature and weather patterns is one of the first steps in selecting the appropriate species for your setting. Different species' temperature and moisture requirements vary, so it's critical to select plants and other organisms that can withstand the typical circumstances in your location. For instance, if you live in a hot, dry area, you should choose plants that can tolerate periods of low rainfall and high temperatures, such as native grasses, cacti, and succulents. On the other hand, shade-loving plants like ferns, mosses, and native woodland species that do well in damp, shadowed conditions can be your best choice if you live in a chilly, humid area.

Another vital thing to consider when selecting species for your environment is the soil type. Different soil parameters, such as pH, nutrient content, and drainage qualities, are preferred by various plants and organisms.

It is imperative that you evaluate your soil to ascertain its composition and fertility before choosing species for your project. Select plants like lavender, rosemary, and yarrow that can thrive in well-drained soil if your soil is sandy or gravelly. Conversely, you can choose to plant plants like hydrangeas, hostas, and astilbes that need damp, fertile soils if your soil is clay or loamy.

When selecting species for your environment, sunlight exposure is yet another crucial factor to consider. While some organisms and plants prefer full or partial shade, others do better in full sun. It's critical to evaluate your site's sunshine circumstances before choosing any species for your project and to ensure the species you choose are compatible with the existing light levels. For instance, you may select sun-loving plants like roses, daylilies, and ornamental grasses if your garden receives a lot of direct sunlight. On the other hand, you can choose to use shade-tolerant plants like hostas, ferns, and coral bells if your wall faces north or has a gloomy spot.

The most important thing to consider when selecting species for your environment is water availability. Because different plants and organisms require different amounts of water, it's critical to choose species that will flourish in your area's natural rainfall patterns or with the irrigation systems you have access to. You may select species with high water requirements, such as bog plants, irises, and water lilies, if you reside in an area with regular rainfall or easy access to water. Succulents, native grasses, and drought-resistant shrubs are examples of drought-tolerant plants that can thrive with little irrigation if you live in a drought-prone location or have restricted access to water.

It's crucial to select species that are appropriate for the project's intended use in addition to taking the surroundings into account. For example, you should choose native species that offer food, shelter, and nesting places for nearby wildlife if you're restoring a natural ecosystem or developing a habitat for wildlife. Compared to foreign or introduced species, native plants and animals are more likely to flourish and maintain natural biodiversity because they are adapted to the particular conditions of your area. However, if you're designing a public garden or building a beautiful garden, consider species based on their visual appeal, blooming periods, and level of maintenance. It's crucial to do your homework and take local ecosystems and biodiversity into account when selecting species for your setting. Invasive or non-native species can potentially upset natural ecosystems, displace native species, and lower biodiversity. It is essential to investigate each species' ecological traits and potential invasiveness before choosing one for your project. Then, pick the species that are least likely to disrupt local ecosystems. Furthermore, you might wish to seek advice on selecting appropriate species for your area from regional specialists like ecologists, botanists, or extension agents.

In conclusion, selecting the appropriate species for your area is critical to developing a biodiverse and sustainable ecosystem that sustains local wildlife as well as human activity. Through careful consideration of variables like soil type, sunshine exposure, water availability, climate, and intended use, You can select species that will thrive in your area and are suited to its particular features. It's also crucial to choose species with the lowest potential for harm and to investigate potential impacts on biodiversity and regional ecosystems. By selecting suitable species and creating resilient ecosystems, you can enhance the aesthetics, utility, and ecological value of your surrounds for future generations.

Indoor vs. Outdoor Cultivation

Plant cultivation, whether for food, medicinal, or ornamental purposes, maybe a gratifying and satisfying experience. However, producers frequently face a quandary when choosing between indoor and outdoor production. Both approaches have advantages and disadvantages, and the final decision is based on criteria such as climate, space availability, resource availability, and personal preferences.

In this post, we'll look at the benefits and drawbacks of indoor and outdoor growing, highlighting the distinct qualities of each method and providing insights to assist producers in making informed decisions.

Indoor production has various benefits, especially for growers who reside in areas with harsh weather or little outdoor space. One of the most significant advantages of indoor output is managing environmental factors such as temperature, humidity, light intensity, and air quality. Growers may achieve optimal growing conditions year-round by utilizing climate control systems, grow lights, and ventilation systems independent of exterior weather conditions. This level of control enables more consistent development and yields, making indoor cultivation suitable for sensitive or high-value crops that demand exact environmental conditions.

Furthermore, indoor growing offers better protection against pests, illnesses, and environmental pressures than outside cultivation. Growing plants indoors reduces the risk of pest infestations, fungal infections, and extreme weather events that can harm or destroy crops. Furthermore, indoor production enables the adoption of integrated pest management (IPM) tactics and organic pest control approaches, which reduces the demand for synthetic pesticides while minimizing environmental effects. This level of control and protection is beneficial for producing high-value crops like cannabis, herbs, and specialty vegetables, which are prone to pests and diseases.

Furthermore, indoor production provides greater privacy, security, and discretion than outdoor cultivation. Growers cultivating plants indoors can hide their activities from neighbors, police enforcement, and possible thieves, lowering the danger of theft, vandalism, or legal ramifications. Furthermore, indoor growth provides greater control over odor, noise, and visibility, making it ideal for growers who want to keep a low profile or adhere to local rules. This level of anonymity and protection is especially crucial for cannabis cultivators and other restricted substance users, who may face legal constraints or societal stigma.

Despite its benefits, indoor cultivation has certain drawbacks, especially regarding resource usage, energy expenses, and environmental impact. Indoor culture takes substantial electricity, water, and nutrients to sustain optimal growing conditions, resulting in higher operating costs and environmental effects than outside cultivation. Furthermore, the usage of artificial lighting and climate control systems can increase energy consumption and greenhouse gas emissions, hastening climate change and environmental deterioration. As a result, some producers may choose outdoor production as a more sustainable and environmentally beneficial option.

On the other hand, outdoor culture has various advantages, especially for growers with adequate outdoor areas and ideal growing circumstances. One of the most significant advantages of outdoor growing is the abundance of natural sunshine, which offers free energy for photosynthesis and encourages healthy plant growth.

Outdoor gardeners can produce high-quality crops with fewer energy inputs and cheaper operational expenses compared to indoor cultivation. Furthermore, outdoor cultivation allows for larger crop quantities, plant diversity, and growing areas, making it ideal for commercial farming and large-scale production.

Furthermore, outdoor culture is more environmentally sustainable and eco-friendly than indoor cultivation because it uses natural resources and relies less on artificial inputs. Growing plants outdoors allows growers to take advantage of natural soil fertility, rainfall, and beneficial microbes, decreasing the need for synthetic fertilizers, pesticides, and irrigation. Outdoor farming enhances biodiversity, ecosystem health, and soil conservation by integrating crops with native vegetation and wildlife habitats. This holistic approach to farming improves ecological resilience and promotes sustainable agriculture methods that benefit both people and the environment.

Furthermore, outdoor gardening provides greater flexibility and versatility than indoor cultivation, allowing for seasonal cropping, crop rotation, and intercropping. Outdoor producers can optimize yields, reduce insect burdens, and increase soil health without the need for artificial interventions by adjusting to seasonal variations and natural cycles. Furthermore, outdoor production offers a more immersive and linked experience with nature, helping farmers to develop a deeper appreciation for the natural world and a stronger bond with the soil. This relationship with nature can be spiritually and emotionally gratifying, instilling a sense of environmental care and duty.

Despite its benefits, outdoor production has certain disadvantages, particularly regarding vulnerability to environmental variables, pests, and illnesses. Outdoor growers are more subject to unpredictable weather occurrences like droughts, floods, frosts, and storms, which can harm or destroy crops and lower harvests. Furthermore, outdoor farming may be vulnerable to pests, illnesses, and wildlife predation, necessitating pest control tactics and preventive measures to protect crops. Furthermore, outdoor cultivation may be constrained by local regulations, zoning limitations, and land use policies that restrict or prohibit specific types of farming activities in urban or suburban regions.

In conclusion, indoor and outdoor growing methods possess benefits and drawbacks, and the choice between them is impacted by factors such as climate, the availability of resources, space, and human preferences. Indoor farming is the best option for growing sensitive or valuable crops year-round since it offers increased control, security, and privacy. On the other hand, compared to outdoor agriculture, indoor cultivation has more resource use, energy costs, and environmental effects. On the other hand, outdoor cultivation provides better sustainability, affordability, and a connection to nature, making it ideal for large-scale production and environmentally responsible farming methods. Finally, the decision between indoor and outdoor growing is based on the grower's aims, priorities, and values, as well as the specific conditions of their environment. Growers can enhance the profitability, sustainability, and enjoyment of their agricultural operations by carefully assessing the benefits and drawbacks of each strategy.

Substrate Selection and Preparation

The selection and preparation of the substrate are essential stages in the culture of various species, such as plants, bacteria, and mushrooms. The substrate, sometimes referred to as the growing medium or growing media, provides the necessary nutrients, water, and structural support for the organisms being grown, acting as the basis for their growth. Selecting the appropriate substrate and correctly preparing it are essential to guarantee the finished product's best possible growth, yield, and quality. We'll examine the nuances of substrate preparation and selection in this section, as well as the variables that affect these procedures and the methods employed to establish optimal growing environments.

The primary factor influencing substrate selection is the particular needs of the grown organism. The substrate must provide the nutrients required for growth and development, as the nutritional requirements of different species vary. For instance, organic substrates like sawdust, straw, or compost are commonly used to grow mushrooms because they offer vital nutrients like nitrogen and carbohydrates. On the other hand, based on their species and stage of growth, plants may require various nutrients. Therefore, the substrate must be customized to suit their unique requirements. The substrate needs to be designed with the unique carbon, nitrogen, and trace element requirements of microorganisms, such as bacteria and fungi, in mind. Growers can choose substrates that promote healthy growth and optimize yields by being aware of the nutritional needs of the target organism.

When selecting a substrate, factors other than nutritional requirements to be taken into account are the substrate's physical and chemical properties. The roughness of the substrate affects aeration and water retention; coarser surfaces provide better drainage and aeration than finer substrates. The moisture content of the substrate is crucial for maintaining the proper hydration levels of the organisms being farmed. Substrates that retain too much water might cause waterlogging, while those that store too little water can cause drought stress. It's crucial to adjust the pH of the substrate to the proper range for the cultivated organisms because it can also affect microbial activity and nutrient availability. Growers can choose substrates that offer the optimal conditions for growth and development by considering these physical and chemical characteristics.

Furthermore, elements like price, availability, and sustainability may have an impact on the choice of substrate. Growers may need to take into account more affordable or easily accessible alternatives to substrates that are more expensive or more difficult to obtain. Furthermore, cultivators could favor locally sourced, recyclable, or renewable substrates in order to reduce their environmental footprint and encourage sustainability. For instance, because they are plentiful, inexpensive, and environmentally friendly, agricultural by-products like rice hulls, maize cobs, and coconut coir are frequently used as mushroom production substrates. Growers can select substrates that fulfill their requirements while lowering expenses and environmental effects by taking these considerations into account.

To produce the best possible environment for growth, the substrate must be carefully prepared after it has been chosen. Sterilization or pasteurization is commonly used in the preparation of substrates in order to get rid of pathogens and competing organisms that can prevent the desired organisms from growing. Sterilization techniques like steam sterilization, autoclaving, or chemical sterilization are frequently employed to eradicate bacteria, fungi, and other microorganisms from the substrate. Although less harsh than sterilization, pasteurization techniques like heat treatment or hot water immersion can nonetheless lower microbial populations and foster the growth of desired species. Growers can minimize the danger of contamination and ensure healthy growth by establishing a clean and safe culture environment through the process of sterilizing or pasteurizing the substrate.

To produce ideal growing conditions, substrate preparation may also include adjusting the nutrient content, pH levels, and moisture content in addition to sterilization or pasteurization. The addition of nutrient supplements, such as supplies of phosphorus, nitrogen, and trace elements, can improve the substrate's nutritional value and encourage rapid development. To bring the pH into the ideal range for the organisms being cultured, alkaline or acidic additives like lime, gypsum, or sulfur can be added. To attain the appropriate moisture content for the cultured organisms, moisture changes can also be done by adding water or compounds that retain moisture. Growers may optimize yields and create the perfect atmosphere for growth by carefully altering these elements.

In order to break down big particles and provide a more homogeneous texture, physical treatments like grinding, chopping, or mixing may also be used during substrate preparation. Substrate texture uniformity is crucial to ensure uniform distribution of air, nutrients, and water throughout the substrate and to encourage uniform growth and production. Physical treatments may also aid in enhancing the structure, porosity, and water retention of the substrate, which will enhance the overall growing environment for the organisms being raised. Growers may establish an environment that promotes healthy root development, uptake of nutrients, and general plant growth by modifying the substrate's texture and structure

In conclusion, choosing and preparing the substrate is a crucial stage in growing a variety of species, such as plants, microbes, and mushrooms. Growers can create an ideal environment for growth and development by correctly preparing substrates that match the target organism's nutritional needs. When choosing a substrate, essential factors to take into account are its physical attributes, pH levels, nutritional content, availability, cost, and sustainability. To produce ideal growing conditions, the preparation of the substrate usually includes adjusting its nutrient content, pH levels, and moisture content in addition to sterilizing or pasteurizing it to get rid of pathogens and competing organisms. Growers can establish an ideal atmosphere for effective production and accomplish their intended results by carefully weighing these aspects and adhering to appropriate preparatory practices.

Inoculation Methods

Vaccination techniques are essential in several disciplines, including microbiology, agriculture, biotechnology, and medicine. In these techniques, microorganisms, including bacteria, fungi, and viruses, are introduced into a substrate or host organism for various applications, including production, research, disease prevention, and environmental cleanup. We examine the ideas, uses, and consequences of the wide range of immunization techniques employed in various contexts for the development of science and inventive practical applications in this section.

Microbiologists use inoculation techniques to investigate microbes' behavior, genetics, and physiology in carefully monitored lab environments. Using a sterile loop or swab, streak plating is a popular technique for inoculation that entails applying a diluted microbial sample to the surface of a solid growth medium in a Petri dish. With the aid of this approach, microbiologists can separate particular colonies of microbes for additional investigation, including genetic modification, antibiotic susceptibility testing, and species identification. In clinical microbiology labs, streak plating is frequently used to diagnose infectious disorders and track antibiotic resistance patterns in bacterial pathogens.

The pour plate technique is another inoculation technique used in microbiology. It entails combining a liquefied agar with a diluted microbial sample and pouring the liquid into a Petri dish. As the agar hardens and traps individual microbial cells, producing colonies throughout the medium, the bacteria in the initial sample can be enumerated and extracted. The pour plate method provides crucial information about the variety, quantity, and dispersion of microorganisms. The pour plate technique offers essential insights into microorganisms' diversity, abundance, and dispersion. It frequently measures bacterial populations in food products, pharmaceutical preparations, and environmental samples.

To improve nutrient cycling, pest management, and crop yield in agricultural contexts, beneficial microbes are introduced into soils, plants, or livestock via inoculation techniques. One such is the symbiotic relationships that nitrogen-fixing bacteria like Rhizobium and Bradyrhizobium create with plant roots to transform atmospheric nitrogen into ammonia, a form that plants may use for growth. This is done by inoculating leguminous crops with these bacteria. Selective strains of nitrogen-fixing bacteria can be injected into legume seedlings to increase nitrogen fixation rates and decrease the demand for synthetic fertilizers, resulting in more ecologically friendly and sustainable farming practices.

Applying mycorrhizal fungus to plant roots is another technique for agricultural inoculation that increases nutrient uptake, resilience, and plant growth. Most land plants' roots create mutualistic relationships with mycorrhizal fungi, which expand their hyphal networks into the soil and increase the surface area available for nutrient absorption. Mycorrhizal fungi can be used to inoculate crops, enhancing the availability of nutrients, water retention, and soil structure. As a result, there may be less need for chemical inputs and more yields and higher-quality products.

In aquaculture, beneficial microbial communities are established and maintained in fish ponds, hatcheries, and aquaponic systems using inoculation techniques. Adding probiotic bacteria or yeast to fish feed or water is a popular inoculation technique that can help with digestion, increase disease resistance, and improve fish health and performance overall. Higher survival rates and improved growth outcomes can be achieved in fish by using probiotic inoculants, such as Bacillus, Lactobacillus, and Saccharomyces, which can selectively eliminate pathogenic bacteria, detoxify toxic substances, and boost immune responses.

Inoculation techniques are used in biotechnology and bioengineering to incorporate genetically engineered microorganisms into industrial processes for the production of medicines, enzymes, biofuels, and other essential goods. Recombinant bacteria or yeast that have been modified to make bioethanol from renewable feedstocks like sugarcane, corn, or lignocellulosic biomass are one example of how fermenters might be inoculated. Biotechnologists can increase bioprocesses' productivity, efficiency, and sustainability by optimizing growth conditions and metabolic pathways. This will pave the way for a bio-based economy that will lessen its need for fossil fuels and help combat climate change.

Inoculation techniques are used in public health and medicine to immunize people against infectious diseases and protect them from pathogens, including viruses, bacteria, and parasites. During vaccination, a pathogen or its antigens are introduced into the body in weakened or dead form to elicit an immune response and produce lifelong protection. Vaccine-induced immunization has been vital in managing and eliminating fatal illnesses like smallpox, polio, measles, and hepatitis, sparing millions of lives and averting immense suffering around the globe.

To sum up, inoculation methods comprise various approaches utilized in biotechnology, medicine, agriculture, and microbiology to introduce microbes into substrates, hosts, or ecosystems for different reasons. Inoculation techniques are crucial tools for scientific research, agricultural innovation, bioproduction, and public health interventions. They can be used to immunize populations against infectious diseases, isolate individual colonies in a Petri dish, or increase crop productivity with beneficial microbes. Scientists and practitioners may address global issues like food security, environmental sustainability, and human health by utilizing the power of microorganisms and their unique capacities, paving the way for a more resilient and promising future for future generations.

Incubation and Fruiting Conditions

The conditions greatly influence the growth, development, and production of mushroom harvests during incubation and fruiting, which are essential components in mushroom agriculture. To produce the perfect environment for mushroom mycelium colonization and fruiting body formation, a variety of parameters, including temperature, humidity, light, ventilation, substrate composition, and microbial activity, must be carefully managed and maximized. This section will examine the significance of incubation and fruiting circumstances in the production of mushrooms, go over the significant variables influencing these conditions, and offer tips on how growers can adjust these variables to get the best results.

A dense network of fungal hyphae is formed when mycelium colonizes the substrate during the incubation phase of mushroom cultivation. Establishing a robust and healthy mycelial network at this phase is essential for facilitating the later development of fruiting bodies. Many variables, including temperature, humidity, substrate moisture content, substrate composition, and microbial activity, affect how well the incubation period goes. To encourage quick mycelial growth, avoid contamination, and guarantee uniform substrate colonization, ideal conditions must be maintained during this phase.

Temperature is one of the most important variables affecting the incubation stage of mushroom cultivation. For the best mycelial growth, mushroom species have different temperature needs; most species prefer temperatures between 20°C and 25°C. The precise temperature range, however, can change based on the strain and species being grown. It's critical to keep steady temperatures within the ideal range to encourage quick mycelial growth and inhibit the growth of rival organisms like bacteria and molds. Temperature variations can potentially hinder mycelium growth in mushrooms and raise the danger of contamination, which can result in low yields and crop loss.

Another crucial element that affects the incubation stage of mushroom cultivation is humidity. High humidity levels are required to preserve the ideal moisture content for mycelial growth and stop moisture loss from the substrate. For most mushroom species, humidity levels between 80% and 90% are commonly advised during incubation. While too much humidity can encourage mold formation and other pollutants, too little moisture can cause the substrate to dry out and limit mycelial growth. Ensuring good mushroom production and fostering an environment conducive to mycelial colonization need careful management of humidity.

In the incubation stage of mushroom cultivation, the substrate moisture content is vital. For mycelial growth and colonization, the substrate needs to be sufficiently moist but not so wet as to be unduly saturated. Excessive moisture content can cause substrates to become anaerobic, which can promote the growth of pathogenic microbes and the generation of hazardous compounds. On the other hand, dry substrates might impede mycelial growth and cause the colonization process to take longer. For the purpose of encouraging quick and consistent mycelial growth and avoiding contamination during the incubation stage, the substrate moisture content must be kept at its ideal level.

The nature of the substrate also influences the incubation stage of mushroom cultivation. Various mushroom species have different substrate needs according to their metabolic and nutritional capacities. Composted organic materials, sawdust, straw, and corn cobs are among the agricultural byproducts that are frequently utilized as substrates for mushroom production. The availability of nutrients, moisture retention, pH levels, and microbial activity are all influenced by the substrate's composition, and these factors, in turn, affect the growth and colonization of mycelial organisms. Maximizing mycelial growth and guaranteeing effective mushroom production depends on knowing the nutritional needs of the target mushroom species and choosing suitable substrates.

When growing mushrooms, the substrate's microbial activity can encourage or prevent mycelial growth during incubation. Beneficial microbes like fungi and bacteria can help break down organic materials, release nutrients, and establish an environment that is favorable for mycelial colonization. However, the mycelium of mushrooms can face competition for resources from pathogenic microbes like molds and bacteria, which can result in contamination and lower yields. Ensuring a clean and sterile environment for mycelial growth and managing microbial activity need careful substrate sterilization or pasteurization. Furthermore, applying chemicals and selective medium can encourage the development of healthy bacteria while blocking the emergence of contaminants.

The fruiting phase of mushroom cultivation starts after the incubation phase, during which environmental factors are changed to encourage the production and growth of fruiting bodies. A number of variables, such as temperature, humidity, light, air movement, and carbon dioxide levels, affect how well the fruiting phase goes. By adjusting these elements, growers can optimize yields and provide ideal circumstances for fruiting body formation.

Temperature is critical in the fruiting phase of mushroom culture because it affects the start, growth, and maturation of fruiting bodies. Certain kinds of mushrooms require a specific temperature to fruit; generally speaking, these species prefer lower temperatures than those during the incubation stage. For fruiting, it is usually advised to keep temperatures between 15°C and 20°C; however, ideal temperature ranges may differ based on the species and strain being grown. Temperature variations can impact the development and creation of fruiting bodies, resulting in atypical growth patterns and decreased yields. Consistent crop production and the promotion of healthy fruiting body formation depend on the proper management of temperature.

Another essential element that affects the fruiting phase of mushroom production is humidity. In order to preserve the ideal moisture content for growth and development and to stop moisture loss from the fruiting bodies, high humidity levels are required. For the majority of mushroom species, humidity levels between 80% and 90% are often advised throughout the fruiting phase. While too much humidity can encourage the spread of mildew and other pollutants, too little moisture might cause the fruiting bodies to dry up and produce fewer fruits. Ensuring good mushroom production and establishing a conducive environment for fruiting body formation need careful humidity management.

Light is a critical environmental component in the fruiting phase of mushroom production, especially for phototropic species like mushrooms. In addition to controlling the onset of fruiting body production, light signals also prevent primordia's creation, elongation, and maturation. Certain species of mushrooms require different amounts of light to fruit; some require light for the production of primordia, while others prefer darkness. Growers must carefully control light intensity, duration, and spectrum in order to maximize yields, as these parameters can all affect the formation and development of fruiting bodies. In indoor growing systems, supplemental lighting can be employed to give more light throughout the fruiting period and encourage consistent production of fruiting bodies.

Air movement is crucial to preserving ideal growing conditions and avoiding carbon dioxide accumulation around fruiting bodies. Enough air circulation creates an atmosphere favorable for the creation and growth of fruiting bodies, encouraging gas exchange, moisture evaporation, and the removal of metabolic byproducts. Carbon dioxide buildup brought on by stagnant air can prevent fruiting body formation and lower yields. A healthy growing environment and good mushroom production depend on adequate ventilation and airflow. Carbon dioxide levels also influence the fruiting phase of mushroom cultivation, as high levels might prevent the production of fruiting bodies.

Common Problems and Solutions

Business, technology, agriculture, or personal growth. Success requires understanding these obstacles and an efficient way to overcome them. This Section will examine industry issues and review possible fixes or mitigation strategies.

Agriculture Unpredictable weather patterns, pest infestations, and degrading soil are just a few of the difficulties farmers confront in this field. Drought is a frequent issue that can seriously lower agricultural yields and jeopardize food security. Farmers can reduce the effects of drought by using water-saving strategies, including mulching, drip irrigation, and rainwater collection. Soil erosion is another prevalent problem that can result in decreased soil fertility and nutrient depletion. Soil erosion can be avoided, and soil health can be preserved by practicing conservation techniques like terracing, cover cropping, and contour plowing. Furthermore, pest infestations are a severe risk to crops, causing losses in yield and financial losses for farmers. Farmers can manage insect populations while reducing environmental damage and maintaining natural ecosystems by implementing integrated pest management (IPM) tactics, which include biological, cultural, and chemical control measures.

Technology businesses frequently need help with cybersecurity, market competition, and product development. One prevalent issue is the speed at which technology develops, making it difficult for businesses to stay competitive and ahead of the curve. To overcome this issue, businesses can invest in research and development (R&D) to continuously innovate and upgrade their products and services. Another common issue is cybersecurity concerns, which include phishing scams, malware attacks, and data breaches. To protect sensitive data from cyberattacks, strong cybersecurity measures like encryption, firewalls, and multi-factor authentication can be put in place.Technological companies, especially startups and small organizations, may need help due to market rivalry. Establishing a distinctive value proposition, cultivating robust client connections, and consistently observing industry developments can assist businesses in standing out from the competition and preserving a competitive advantage.

Business Organizations in the business sector deal with various issues pertaining to staff management, financing, and operations. Businesses frequently need help with cash flow management, which involves keeping sufficient cash reserves to pay for. There will inevitably be difficulties and roadblocks in every undertaking, whether operating costs or fulfilling financial commitments. By implementing good financial planning, budgeting, and cash flow forecasting techniques, firms can improve their financial management and steer clear of cash flow issues. Employee turnover is another prevalent problem that can cause delays in workflow, lower productivity, and higher recruitment expenses. Businesses may recruit and retain top talent by implementing employee retention measures like competitive salaries, opportunities for professional development, and a healthy work culture. Additionally, businesses—tiny and medium-sized firms (SMEs)—may face difficulties due to market volatility and economic uncertainty. Businesses may handle economic downturns and lessen the impact of market volatility by creating backup plans, diversifying their revenue sources, and preserving good connections with suppliers and consumers.

Personal growth People frequently need help with self-control, goal-setting, and time management in their personal development. Procrastination, the tendency to put off or postpone crucial or necessary chores, is one prevalent issue. One way to beat procrastination is to divide work into smaller, more manageable pieces, set goals and deadlines, and establish a conducive environment that reduces outside noise and promotes concentration and productivity. Lack of motivation, or the inability to muster the will and vigor to follow one's dreams, is another prevalent problem. People can identify the intrinsic drive, set attainable goals, and enlist the assistance of friends, family, or mentors to help them stay motivated and focused on their personal development journey. Furthermore, effective time management might improve productivity and personal development. People can more effectively manage their time and accomplish their goals by implementing time management strategies, such as prioritizing activities, establishing limits, and using calendars and to-do lists.

In conclusion, joint issues and difficulties will always arise in various industries, such as business, technology, agriculture, and personal development. However, people and organizations can overcome challenges, accomplish goals, and succeed in their respective pursuits by comprehending the underlying reasons for these issues and putting effective solutions into place. Proactive problem-solving and continual improvement are crucial for success in every profession, whether putting novel cybersecurity measures in place for the technology industry, enhancing time management skills for personal development, or implementing water conservation practices on farms.

CHAPTER III

Mushroom Species Profiles

Button Mushrooms (Agaricus bisporus)

One of the most popular mushroom species in the world for cultivation and consumption is the button mushroom (Agaricus bisporus), which is prized for its many health advantages, adaptable culinary uses, and mild flavor. Known by several names such as champignon or white mushrooms, they are a commercial cultivar of the Agaricus species grown in many nations in Europe, North America, and Asia. This section will examine button mushrooms' traits, production techniques, nutritional makeup, culinary applications, and health advantages. It will also discuss the importance of button mushrooms to the world's mushroom market and how they contribute to human health and well-being.

When fully grown, button mushrooms typically have a 2 to 5 centimeters diameter. This small to medium size is what distinguishes them from other mushrooms. They have tightly closed gills behind their spherical crown, which has a smooth, creamy-white surface. The gills may turn pink to brown, and the caps may flatten as the mushrooms age. The flesh is soft and creamy-white, while the stems are firm and white with a little fibrous feel. Button mushrooms are adaptable ingredients in various culinary preparations because of their gentle, earthy flavor with faint nutty undertones

Button mushroom cultivation is an extraordinarily rigorous and controlled procedure that calls for meticulous control over the growth parameters and specialized climatic conditions. The substrate production, which acts as the nutrient-rich growing media for mushrooms, usually marks the start of the culture phase. Straw, horse dung, and chicken litter are examples of composted agricultural materials frequently utilized as substrates for button mushroom development.

The substrate is pasteurized or sterilized to eradicate rival microorganisms and create a sterile atmosphere suitable for the colonization of mushroom mycelium.

After the substrate is ready, it is injected with mushroom spawn, made out of a substrate that has been colonized by mycelium from mushrooms. The substrate and spawn are well combined and then uniformly divided among trays or beds. To encourage mycelial growth and colonization, the inoculated substrate is subsequently placed in a controlled environment with particular humidity, temperature, and ventilation levels. To start the creation of fruiting bodies, a layer of casing material, such as vermiculite or peat moss, is placed on the substrate once the mycelium has wholly colonized it.

In the fruiting stage, button mushrooms progressively grow into mature mushrooms throughout one to two weeks, starting as tiny pinheads that poke out of the casing layer. When the mushrooms reach the button stage—when the gills are still immature and white—they are manually harvested. Harvesting at this point guarantees the best possible flavor, texture, and look. The mushrooms are graded, cleaned, and packed after harvesting in preparation for delivery to customers, restaurants, and markets.
In addition to being tasty, button mushrooms are rich in nutrients, including a range of vitamins, minerals, and bioactive substances that support general well-being.

They're also a great source of fiber, potassium, phosphorus, selenium, protein, and vitamins B and D. Substances found in button mushrooms include beta- glucans, polysaccharides, and antioxidants. These substances have been connected to a number of health advantages, such as immune system support, anti- inflammatory properties, and defense against chronic illnesses, including cancer and cardiovascular disease.

Button mushrooms are pretty adaptable in the kitchen and can be used as a topping for pizza, pasta dishes, stir-fries, and soups and salads. They cook well through sautéing, grilling, roasting, and stuffing, and their mild flavor goes well with various other components. Button mushrooms enhance the taste and texture of food by combining nicely with herbs, garlic, onions, cheese, and meats.

Button mushrooms have been utilized for millennia ifor their alleged health benefits as well as its culinary uses in traditional medical systems like Ayurveda and Traditional Chinese Medicine (TCM). They are used to support energy, longevity, and general well-being and are said to have tonic and immune-boosting qualities. Many of these traditional uses have been confirmed by contemporary scientific study, which also affirms the health-promoting properties of button mushrooms and their bioactive components.

To sum up, button mushrooms are a highly sought-after and extensively grown type of mushroom appreciated for their mild flavor, a plethora of culinary uses, and several health advantages. They are widely used in traditional medicine and international cuisine and farmed commercially in many nations. Button mushrooms have a delectable flavor, are high in nutrients, and may have health advantages that will make them a mainstay in diets and kitchens for many generations to come.

Shiitake (Lentinula edodes)

Shiitake mushrooms (Lentinula edodes) are a highly valued and respected mushroom species with a long and illustrious history spanning thousands of years. Shiitake mushrooms are native to East Asia, specifically Japan, China, and Korea. They have been farmed and eaten for generations due to their unique flavor, adaptability in the kitchen, and certain health advantages. We shall delve into the intriguing world of shiitake mushrooms in this extensive Sentence, going over its traits, cultivation techniques, nutritional profile, culinary applications, medicinal qualities, and cultural significance.

The distinctive feature of shiitake mushrooms is their big, umbrella-shaped caps, which come in various colors from light to dark brown. The smooth, velvety surface of the caps and the conspicuous gills on the underside give them a unique touch. The flesh is juicy and soft with a fibrous texture and thick, complex, and woody stems. With elements of earthiness and smoke, shiitake mushrooms have a deep, savory flavor frequently characterized as meaty or umami. They are highly regarded for their distinct taste and adaptability in the kitchen, which makes them a favorite component in many different recipes, including pasta dishes, risottos, stir-fries, soups, and meat alternatives for vegetarian and vegan diets.

Shiitake mushroom cultivation is a specialist procedure that calls for specific environmental requirements and cautious control of growing parameters. Logs or stumps of broadleaf trees, including oak, beech, chestnut, and maple, were traditionally used to grow shiitake mushrooms through a process called "forest cultivation" or "log cultivation." After being injected with shiitake spawn—a substrate that has been infected with mycelium—the logs are left to incubate for many months in a damp, darkened space. The logs are placed in outdoor mushroom beds or stacked in racks to encourage fruiting once the mycelium has wholly colonized them.

Shiitake mushrooms are also grown on logs. However, alternate techniques, including sawdust, enhanced sawdust, and synthetic substrate growth, are also used to produce them. In sawdust cultivation, shiitake spawn is injected into sterilized sawdust, and the substrate is then cultivated under carefully monitored conditions in trays or bags. To improve nutrient availability and promote mycelial growth, supplements like wheat bran, rice bran, or soybean meal are added to the sawdust substrate during the supplemented sawdust culture process. For shiitake culture, synthetic substrate cultivation uses artificial materials like straw, maize cobs, or cottonseed hulls as the substrate. This method allows for more flexibility and control over the growing environment.

In addition to being tasty, shiitake mushrooms are very nutrient-dense, providing a variety of vitamins, minerals, and bioactive substances that support general health and well-being. They are a great source of fiber, potassium, phosphorus, zinc, and vitamins B and D. They are also high in protein. Additionally, bioactive substances found in shiitake mushrooms include polysaccharides, beta-glucans, and ergosterol. These substances have been connected to several health advantages, such as immune system support, anti-inflammatory effects, and cholesterol-lowering qualities. Furthermore, antioxidants like ergothioneine and selenium, which help shield cells from oxidative damage and lower Shiitake mushrooms carry a high risk of chronic ailments, including cancer and cardiovascular disease.

For centuries, shiitake mushrooms have been valued for their therapeutic qualities and employed in the treatment of many illnesses in conventional medical systems such as Traditional Chinese Medicine (TCM) and Japanese Kampo. They are used to increase vigor, fortify the immune system, and encourage longevity. They are thought to have tonic and immunological-enhancing qualities. Numerous of these traditional applications have been validated by contemporary scientific study, which shows the medicinal potential of shiitake mushrooms in preventing and treating a range of medical disorders. Research has indicated that shiitake mushrooms possess antibacterial, antiviral, and anticancer properties and positively affect blood pressure, cholesterol, and sugar levels.

Shiitake mushrooms are highly adaptable in the kitchen and may be used to add depth of provide taste, texture, and nutrients to a variety of dishes. They are perfect for stir-fries, soups, stews, risotto, and pasta dishes because of their meaty texture and rich, umami flavor, which go well with various other ingredients. Shiitake mushrooms go well with herbs, garlic, onions, ginger, soy sauce, and sesame oil. They can be cooked in a variety of methods, including roasting, grilling, braising, and sautéing. They provide a tasty substitute for animal protein and are frequently used in vegetarian and vegan cuisine.

Shiitake mushrooms have cultural significance in East Asian cuisines and traditions, in addition to their culinary and medical purposes. They are frequently offered during festive festivities and special occasions since they are treasured as a sign of longevity, health, and fortune. In Japan, shiitake mushrooms are common in bento boxes, sushi, and traditional foods, including miso soup, nabemono (hot pot), and nimono (simmered dishes). Shiitake mushrooms are highly valued in China for their culinary and therapeutic qualities, and they are frequently added to soups, stir-fries, and braised meals. In Korea, shiitake mushrooms are commonly used in traditional medicinal treatments, kimchi, jjigae (stew), and bulgogi (grilled meat).

To sum up, shiitake mushrooms are a highly sought-after and adaptable type of fungus that are appreciated for their unique flavor, adaptability in the kitchen, and possible health advantages. Their delectable flavor and nutritious content have drawn people from all over the world to them since they were first cultivated and consumed in East Asia millennia ago. For many centuries to come, shiitake mushrooms will undoubtedly be a prized element in kitchens, cuisines, and civilizations due to their rich history, many applications, and medicinal qualities.

Oyster Mushrooms (Pleurotus spp.)

Pleurotus spp., or oyster mushrooms, are a varied species of edible fungi highly valued for their many health advantages, distinctive look, and mild flavor. As members of the Pleurotus genus, which also includes species like Pleurotus ostreatus, Pleurotus pulmonarius, and Pleurotus eryngii, oyster mushrooms are grown and eaten all over the world because of their nutritional worth and versatility in the kitchen. This in-depth sentence will examine the traits, production techniques, nutritional makeup, culinary applications, health benefits, and environmental advantages of oyster mushrooms, emphasizing their importance to the world's mushroom trade and their function in advancing ecological sustainability and human health.

The oyster-shaped caps of oyster mushrooms are distinctive and can be white, light brown, gray, or pink, depending on the species and growth environment. The velvety-textured caps might be smooth or slightly wrinkled, with gills extending the stem's entire length. The flesh is luscious, soft, and has a moderate flavor. The stems are short, thick, and centered on the cap. Oyster mushrooms have a firm, meaty texture that holds up well when cooked and a delicate, sweet flavor that is reminiscent of shellfish, thus the name. They are highly valued for their adaptability in the kitchen because they go well with various dishes and have several preparation options.

Oyster mushroom cultivation is a reasonably easy process that may be carried out on a modest scale with essential tools and materials. The substrate that oyster mushrooms are grown on offers the mushrooms a nutrient-rich habitat in which to grow. Agricultural leftovers, including straw, corn cobs, and cottonseed hulls, are frequently used as oyster mushroom cultivation substrates. Sawdust, coffee grounds, and cardboard are also common materials. In order to eradicate rival microorganisms and create a sterile atmosphere suitable for the colonization of mushroom mycelium, the substrate is pasteurized or sterilized.

After the substrate is ready, it is injected with oyster mushroom spawn, which is either grain or substrate that has been infected with mycelium. The substrate and spawn are well combined and then evenly divided into trays, bags, or other containers. To encourage mycelial growth and colonization, the inoculated substrate is after that, put in a dark, humid environment with particular temperature and ventilation requirements. Pinheads start to appear after the mycelium has completely colonized the substrate, and they will eventually grow into adult mushrooms in one to two weeks. To achieve the best possible flavor, texture, and look, oyster mushrooms are usually hand-harvested during the button stage, when the gills are still white and underdeveloped, and the caps are still securely closed.

In addition to being tasty, oyster mushrooms are also exceptionally nutrient-dense, containing various vitamins, minerals, and bioactive substances that support general health and wellbeing. They are a great source of fiber, potassium, phosphorus, iron, and vitamins B and D. They are also high in protein. Additionally, bioactive substances found in oyster mushrooms include beta-glucans, polysaccharides, and antioxidants. These substances have been connected to a number of health advantages, such as immune system support, anti-inflammatory properties, and defense against chronic illnesses, including cancer and cardiovascular disease. Oyster mushrooms are an excellent option for anyone trying to maintain a healthy diet and way of life because they are also low in calories, fat, and cholesterol.

When it comes to cooking, oyster mushrooms are highly adaptable and can be utilized to enhance flavor, texture, and nutritional value in a wide range of meals. They are excellent for sautéing, stir-frying, grilling, roasting, and braising because of their firm, meaty texture and delicate, sweet flavor. Oyster mushrooms go well with meats, seafood, poultry, and other vegetables. They also go well with herbs, garlic, onions, ginger, soy sauce, and sesame oil. They are frequently used as a meat alternative in vegetarian and vegan recipes, as well as in soups, stews, risotto, pasta meals, and veggie side dishes.

Oyster mushrooms have been utilized for millennia in both for their culinary uses and their purported health benefits, ancient medical systems like Ayurveda and ancient Chinese Medicine (TCM). They are used to increase vigor, fortify the immune system, and encourage longevity. They are thought to have tonic and immunological-enhancing qualities. Many of these traditional uses have been validated by contemporary scientific study, which shows oyster mushrooms have medicinal promise in the prevention and treatment of a wide range of health disorders. Studies have proven oyster mushrooms to have positive benefits on blood pressure, cholesterol, and sugar levels in addition to antibacterial, antiviral, and anticancer properties.

Oyster mushrooms provide a number of sustainability advantages that make them a desirable choice for growers and consumers who care about the environment. Because oyster mushrooms grow quickly and have a sizeable potential production, space, and resources may be used effectively. They may be grown on various agricultural waste products and residues, such as cardboard, sawdust, straw, and coffee grounds. This lowers the demand for virgin materials and keeps organic waste out of landfills. Furthermore, because oyster mushrooms are effective decomposers, they can be utilized in bioremediation to remove toxins and organic pollutants from soil and water, improving the sustainability of the environment and the health of ecosystems.

To sum up, oyster mushrooms are a rich and adaptable type of mushroom that are prized for their mild flavor, adaptability in the kitchen, and possible health advantages. Because of their distinct taste and texture, as well as their medicinal qualities and advantages for sustainability, they are grown and consumed all over the world. Oyster mushrooms are sure to be a cherished component in kitchens, cuisines, and cultures for many generations to come because of their lengthy history, wide range of applications, and significant health and environmental advantages.

Morel Mushrooms (Morchella spp.)

Morel mushrooms, or Morchella spp., are elusive and highly valued mushrooms that are coveted for their unique look, flavor, and culinary adaptability. Chefs, foragers, and connoisseurs of mushrooms all have a strong need for morel mushrooms. They are members of the genus Morchella, which also includes species including Morchella conica, elata, and esculenta. This in-depth study will examine the traits, environment, production techniques, nutritional makeup, culinary applications, health benefits, and cultural significance of morel mushrooms, illuminating their attraction and relevance within the realm of fungus.

The distinctive honeycomb-like caps of morel mushrooms are pitted, hollow, and have deep ridges and valleys. Depending on the species and growing circumstances, the caps' color can vary from light beige to dark brown or black. They are joined to a central stem. Usually pale and fibrous, the flesh is delicate, spongy, and porous, and the stems have a hollow center. When cooked, morel mushrooms maintain their meaty texture and develop a deep, earthy flavor with subtle nutty undertones. They are widely sought-after as an ingredient in gourmet cooking due to their unique taste and scent, which only gets better when cooked.

Morel mushrooms are native to temperate regions of the Northern Hemisphere, and they are usually found in woodlands, meadows, and wooded areas with well-drained soil and a lot of organic matter. They often emerge in the spring, as soon as the ground thaws and the temperature rises. Although they can also be found in other settings like burned areas, riverbanks, and disturbed soils, morel mushrooms are frequently linked to particular tree species, such as ash, elm, oak, and poplar.

With their host trees, morel mushrooms create symbiotic relationships known as mycorrhizal associations, which are advantageous to both the fungi and the trees.

Since morel mushrooms have a complicated life cycle and specific ecological requirements, growing them is known to be extremely difficult and has prevented effective commercialization for many years. In contrast to numerous other types of mushrooms that can be grown using standardized techniques and materials, morel mushrooms need certain environmental circumstances and mycorrhizal relationships with host trees in order to flourish. Indoor cultivation of morel mushrooms with artificial substrates and regulated surroundings has yet to be largely successful due to the fungi's inability to fruit or generate viable spores in artificial environments. Therefore, the main method used to gather morel mushrooms is by foragers and mushroom hunters who use their understanding of the local ecosystems, soil types, and weather patterns to identify and gather these elusive fungus from their native habitat. In many areas, morel hunting has become a popular past time and cultural practice, with aficionados looking forward to springtime and the opportunity to hunt for these highly sought-after mushrooms in the wild. Trekking through forests and woodlands to look for evidence of morel mushrooms sprouting from the soil and leaf litter is a common method of morel hunting.

In addition to being delicious, morel mushrooms are very nutrient-dense, providing a variety of vitamins, minerals, and bioactive substances that support general health and wellbeing. They are a great source of fiber, potassium, phosphorus, iron, and vitamins B and D. They are also high in protein. Bioactive substances found in morel mushrooms include antioxidants, polysaccharides, and phenolic compounds. These substances have been connected to several health advantages, such as immune system support, anti-inflammatory properties, and defense against chronic illnesses like cancer and cardiovascular disease. Morel mushrooms are a wholesome and nutrient-dense because they are minimal in fat and calories, they are a great compliment to any diet.

In the culinary arts, morel mushrooms are prized for their distinct flavor and aroma, which improve and add richness and depth to a wide range of cuisines. They work well in soups, sauces, risotto, pasta meals, and desserts, as well as savory and sweet recipes. Morel mushrooms can be prepared in a number of ways, such as sautéing, frying, grilling, roasting, and braising. They also go well with various ingredients, such as herbs, garlic, onions, shallots, cream, butter, wine, and cheese. Morel mushrooms are a delicacy in many cultures and are frequently used in fine dining, fetching high rates in markets and dining establishments.

Since ancient times, morel mushrooms have been utilized for their alleged therapeutic benefits in Native American herbalism and Traditional Chinese Medicine (TCM), in addition to its culinary applications. They are used to cure various illnesses, such as weariness, digestive problems, and respiratory infections. It is thought that they contain tonic and immune-boosting qualities. Numerous of these traditional applications have been validated by contemporary scientific study, which shows the medicinal potential of morel mushrooms in the prevention and treatment of a range of medical disorders. Research has demonstrated that morel mushrooms have positive impacts on blood sugar, cholesterol, and immune system function in addition to their antibacterial, antioxidant, and anti-inflammatory properties.

To sum up, morel mushrooms are an elusive and highly sought-after species of fungus that are appreciated for their unique flavor, adaptability in the kitchen, and certain health advantages. Because of their distinct taste and scent, chefs and gourmet food fans highly prize these mushrooms, which are collected by foragers and mushroom hunters from their natural habitat. Morel mushrooms continue to pique the interest of mushroom lovers and outdoor enthusiasts everywhere due to their fascinating life cycle, rich history, and cultural significance.

Porcini Mushrooms (Boletus edulis)

One of the most admired and sought-after wild mushroom species is porcini (Boletus edulis), which is valued for its rich flavor, meaty texture, and culinary adaptability. Porcini mushrooms, which are a common element in traditional European cuisine, are highly valued in gastronomy and belong to the Boletus genus, which also includes numerous closely related species. We shall examine the traits, environment, production techniques, nutritional makeup, culinary applications, health benefits, and cultural significance of porcini mushrooms in this in-depth study, emphasizing their attraction and relevance within the realm of fungi.

Large, thick, meaty caps that vary in color from light brown to dark brown or chestnut, depending on the age and maturity of the mushroom, are what define porcini mushrooms. The caps are coated in a network of tiny scales or dots and are often convex when young, becoming flat or slightly concave as they age. When the cap is young, its small, angular pores or tubes are white or yellow, but as it ages, it turns greenish-yellow or olive-brown. The underside of the cap is porous. Thick, robust, and frequently bulbous at the base, the stems have a creamy-white to pale brown coloring. The solid, meaty texture of porcini mushrooms and their rich, earthy flavor with nutty undertones stand up well when cooked.

Porcini mushrooms grow alongside several tree species, including oak, chestnut, beech, and pine, and are native to temperate parts of Europe, North America, and Asia. They are usually found in mountainous areas, woodlands, and mixed forests that have lots of organic matter and well-drained soil. Porcini mushrooms and their host trees develop symbiotic relationships through a mycorrhizal interaction that is advantageous to both parties. While the trees give the mushrooms carbohydrates and other nutrients, the mushrooms assist the trees in absorbing water and nutrients from the soil.

Because of its complicated life cycle and habitat requirements, porcini mushroom cultivation is renowned for being difficult and has yet to be successfully commercialized. In contrast to numerous other types of mushrooms that may be grown with uniform techniques and materials, porcini mushrooms need particular environmental circumstances and mycorrhizal relationships with host trees in order to flourish. Porcini mushrooms are a difficult fungus to grow indoors; even with artificial substrates and regulated conditions, the fungus frequently fails to fruit or generate viable spores.

Because of this, porcini mushrooms are mainly collected from their natural habitat by foragers and mushroom hunters. These individuals identify and gather this valuable fungus by using their knowledge of the area's ecosystems, soil types, and weather patterns. In many areas, the pursuit of porcini mushrooms in the wild has grown to be a popular past time and cultural practice, with aficionados looking forward to autumn and the opportunity to go mushroom hunting. Trekking through forests and woodlands to look for evidence of porcini mushrooms sprouting from the soil and leaf litter is a standard method of porcini hunting.

In addition to being tasty, porcini mushrooms are very nutrient-dense, providing a variety of vitamins, minerals, and bioactive substances that support general health and wellbeing. They're also a great source of fiber, potassium, phosphorus, selenium, vitamins B and D, and protein. Additionally, bioactive substances found in porcini mushrooms include antioxidants, polysaccharides, and beta-glucans. These substances have been connected to a number of health advantages, including immune system support, anti-inflammatory properties, and defense against chronic illnesses, including cancer and cardiovascular disease. Porcini mushrooms are a wholesome and nutrient-dense supplement to any diet because they are also low in calories and fat.

Porcini mushrooms are widely valued in the culinary world for their unique flavor and scent, which enhance a variety of recipes and give them depth and complexity. They work well in soups, sauces, risotto, pasta dishes, and pies, among other savory and sweet recipes. Porcini mushrooms can be prepared in a number of ways, such as sautéing, frying, grilling, roasting, and braising. They also go well with a wide range of ingredients, such as herbs, garlic, onions, shallots, cream, butter, wine, and cheese. Porcini mushrooms are prized in many cultures as a delicacy and are frequently used in fine dining settings, where they fetch high prices in markets and dining establishments.

Apart from their culinary use, porcini mushrooms have been utilized for their alleged therapeutic qualities in traditional medicine systems such as European herbalism and Traditional Chinese Medicine (TCM) for millennia. They cure various illnesses, such as tiredness, respiratory infections, and digestive issues. It is thought that they have tonic and immune-enhancing qualities. Numerous of these traditional applications have been validated by contemporary scientific study, which shows the medicinal potential of porcini mushrooms in the prevention and treatment of a range of medical disorders. Research has demonstrated that porcini mushrooms have positive impacts on blood sugar, cholesterol, and immune system function in addition to their antibacterial, antioxidant, and anti-inflammatory properties.

Porcini mushrooms are revered as a symbol of wealth, success, and good fortune in European cuisine and folklore, giving them a unique cultural significance. They appear in regional specialties like porcini mushroom soup, stuffed porcini mushrooms, and porcini mushroom sauces, as well as in classic recipes like cotoletta alla bolognese con porcini, tagliatelle al Tartufo e porcini, and risotto ai funghi porcini. Additionally, porcini mushrooms are often used in Italian and French cooking as an ingredient to enhance the flavor of sauces, stews, and braises. They can also be used in soups and stocks in a dry form to offer more flavor depth.

To sum up, porcini mushrooms are an elusive and highly sought-after type of mushroom that are appreciated for their meaty texture, rich flavor, and versatility in cooking. Because of their distinct taste and scent, chefs and gourmet food fans highly prize these mushrooms, which are collected by foragers and mushroom hunters from their natural habitat. Porcini mushrooms continue to awe and enthrall mushroom lovers and nature lovers everywhere because of their intricate life cycle, nutritional worth, and cultural significance.

Enoki Mushrooms (Flammulina velutipes)

The delicate and unusual enoki mushroom species (Flammulina velutipes) is distinguished by its long, thin stems and tiny, button-like caps. Enoki mushrooms, which are members of the Flammulina species, are highly valued for their crunchy texture and mild, slightly fruity flavor. As a result, they are a favorite among mushroom fans worldwide and are often used as a component of Asian cuisine. To shed light on the appeal and significance of enoki mushrooms in the realm of fungi, we shall examine their traits, habitat, cultivation techniques, nutritional profile, culinary applications, medicinal qualities, and cultural relevance in this extensive study.

Enoki mushrooms are distinguished by their small, round caps, which are often creamy white or pale yellow in color, and their extended, pencil-thin stems, which can reach lengths of several inches. The stems are robust, fibrous, and white, while the crowns are somewhat convex in shape and may darken with age. With a crunchy texture that holds its crispness even after cooking, enoki mushrooms have a mild, slightly fruity flavor that is evocative of fresh radishes or sweet corn. They are highly regarded for their delicate flavor and distinctive look, which provide a variety of foods with more visual appeal and texture.

Enoki mushrooms are native to East Found in temperate regions of China, Japan, Korea, and Taiwan, it grows on rotting hardwood trees and stumps in forests and woodlands. Additionally, they are grown for profit in regulated settings using specific growing methods and substrates. Enoki mushrooms grow best in cool, humid environments Within 10 to 20°C (50 to 68°F) is the best temperature range for greenhouses and indoor mushroom farms.

Enoki mushroom cultivation is a complex procedure that calls for certain environmental requirements and cautious control of growing parameters. The growing of enoki mushrooms was traditionally done on sawdust blocks or logs, a technique called "forest cultivation" or "log cultivation." In order to encourage mycelial growth and fruiting, sawdust blocks or logs were inoculated with enoki mushroom spawn, which is a mycelium-infused substrate. They were then placed in a humid, shady setting. Pinheads started to appear when the mycelium had colonized entirely the substrate, and these finally turned into mature mushrooms with long, thin stems and tiny, button-like caps.

Apart from the conventional techniques, other methods such as sawdust bag, bottle, and jar cultivation are also employed to develop enoki mushrooms. In sawdust bag cultivation, enoki mushroom spawn is injected into sterilized sawdust-filled bags, and the bags are then incubated in a controlled atmosphere until the mushrooms are ready to be harvested. Jar cultivation involves the inoculation of glass jars containing sterilized substrate, whereas bottle cultivation uses plastic bottles or containers loaded with the same substance. Enoki mushrooms can be grown all year round using these techniques, which provide more flexibility and control over the growing environment despite seasonal differences.

In addition to being delicious, enoki mushrooms are quite nutritional, providing a variety of vitamins, minerals, and bioactive substances that support general health and wellbeing. They're also a great source of fiber, potassium, phosphorus, selenium, vitamins B and D, and protein. Bioactive substances found in enoki mushrooms, such as polysaccharides, beta-glucans, and antioxidants, have also been related to a number of health advantages, such as immune system support, anti-inflammatory properties, and defense against chronic illnesses like cancer and cardiovascular disease. Enoki mushrooms are a wholesome and nutrient-dense because they are minimal in fat and calories, they are a great compliment to any diet.

Enoki mushrooms are extremely adaptable in the kitchen and can be utilized to enhance flavor, texture, and nutritional value in a wide range of meals. They work well in stir-fries, soups, salads, sushi rolls, and hot pot recipes because of their mild, somewhat fruity flavor and crisp texture. Raw or cooked enoki mushrooms complement a wide range of foods, including fish, meats, tofu, veggies, and noodles. They are frequently added to food as a garnish or topper, giving the dish a lovely, light flavor and aesthetic appeal.

Beyond their culinary applications, enoki mushrooms have been utilized for generations in traditional medicine systems such as Japanese Kampo and Traditional Chinese Medicine (TCM) due to their supposed therapeutic qualities. They are used to cure various illnesses, such as weariness, digestive problems, and respiratory infections. It is thought that they contain tonic and immune-boosting qualities. Many of these traditional uses have been validated by contemporary scientific study, which shows the medicinal potential of enoki mushrooms in the prevention and treatment of various medical disorders. Research has indicated that enoki mushrooms possess antibacterial, Along with their positive benefits on blood sugar management, cholesterol levels, and immune system function, they also have anti-inflammatory and antioxidant qualities.

From a cultural standpoint, enoki mushrooms are revered in Asian cooking and culinary customs as a representation of longevity, wealth, and good fortune. They can be found in a variety of traditional dishes, including sushi rolls, noodle soups, stir-fries, and hot pots, as well as in celebratory dishes for celebrations and special events. Enoki mushrooms are thought to enhance health and energy, which is why they are frequently employed in herbal cures and traditional medicine preparations. Enoki mushrooms are used in stir-fries and hot pot dishes in China, but they are also frequently served in miso soup and as a topping for grilled meats and vegetables in Japan.

To sum up, enoki mushrooms are a special kind of fungus that may be used in a variety of ways. They are prized for their crunchy texture, mild flavor, and high nutritional content. They are grown and eaten all over the world for their cultural significance and symbolism, as well as for their culinary diversity and possible health advantages. Owing to their unique flavor, texture, and look, enoki mushrooms are a popular element in cuisines and cultures all over the world, stimulating culinary innovation and capturing the mind of foodies.

Lion's Mane (Hericium erinaceus)

Hericium erinaceus, sometimes known as the "Lion's Mane" mushroom, is a unique and uncommon species prized for its odd appearance, remarkable medicinal qualities, and variety of culinary uses. The Lion's Mane mushroom, sometimes called the "pom pom mushroom" or the "bearded tooth mushroom," gets its name from its shaggy, white, cascading spines that resemble a lion's mane. Lion's Mane mushrooms, which are members of the Hericium genus, are becoming more and more well-known in Western cuisine and wellness practices. They have long been valued for their possible therapeutic benefits in traditional Asian medicine. To shed light on the relevance of Lion's Mane mushrooms in the realm of fungus, we will examine its traits, habitat, cultivation techniques, nutritional profile, culinary applications, medicinal qualities, and cultural meaning in this extensive study.

Lion's mane mushrooms are found on the decaying wood of hardwood trees such as birch, oak, beech, and maple. They are indigenous to Asia, Europe, and North America's temperate zones. They can be found in old-growth forests, woodlands, and mountainous regions. They are usually spotted in late summer or early fall. In symbiotic relationships that are advantageous to both the fungi and the trees, Lion's Mane mushrooms have a mycorrhizal interaction with their host trees. While the trees give the mushrooms carbohydrates and other nutrients, the mushrooms assist the trees in absorbing water and nutrients from the soil.

The increased interest in Lion's Mane mushrooms' possible health advantages and culinary applications has led to a rise in popularity for their cultivation in recent years. In contrast to numerous other types of mushrooms that are grown on materials like grain or sawdust, Lion's Mane mushrooms are usually grown on hardwood logs or blocks using a process called "forest cultivation" or "log cultivation." To encourage mycelial growth and fruiting, the logs or blocks are inoculated with Lion's Mane mushroom spawn, which is a mycelium-infused substrate, and then incubated in a humid, shady location. Lion's Mane mushrooms start to emerge after the mycelium has completely colonized the substrate. Eventually, these mushrooms mature and develop cascading spines.

Other methods besides log cultivation that can be used to develop Lion's Mane mushrooms include sawdust bag cultivation, bottle cultivation, and jar cultivation. These techniques entail adding Lion's Mane mushroom spawn to sterilized substrate-filled bags, bottles, or jars and incubating them in a regulated environment until the mushrooms are ready to be harvested. Because of the increased flexibility and control over growing circumstances provided by these cultivation techniques, Lion's Mane mushrooms can be grown year-round, regardless of seasonal fluctuations.

In addition to being tasty, Lion's Mane mushrooms are also exceptionally nutrient-dense, containing a variety of vitamins, minerals, and bioactive substances that support general health and wellbeing. They're also a great source of fiber, potassium, phosphorus, selenium, vitamins B and D, and protein. Bioactive substances found in lion's mane mushrooms, such as polysaccharides, hericenones, and antioxidants, have also been connected to a number of health advantages, including immune system support, improved cognition, and nerve regeneration. Lion's Mane mushrooms are a wholesome and nutrient-dense because they are minimal in fat and calories, they are a great compliment to any diet.

When it comes to cooking, Lion's Mane mushrooms are quite adaptable and may be used in a wide range of meals, contributing taste, texture, and nutrients. They have a meaty, soft texture that holds up well when cooked and a mild, somewhat sweet flavor that is suggestive of seafood or shellfish. Lion's Mane mushrooms are a popular meat substitute in vegan and vegetarian cooking. They can be grilled, roasted, stir-fried, sautéed, or braised. They work nicely in soups, stews, pasta recipes, risotto, salad dressings, and with garlic, onions, herbs, butter, wine, and cream, among other things.

Lion's Mane mushrooms are used in traditional medicine systems like Japanese Kampo and Traditional Chinese Medicine (TCM) for their purported medicinal benefits in addition to their culinary uses. They are used to treat a range of conditions, such as nervous system problems, cognitive decline, and digestive issues. It is thought that they have tonic and adaptogenic qualities. Numerous of these traditional applications have been validated by contemporary scientific study, which shows the medicinal potential of Lion's Mane mushrooms in the prevention as well as the management of other medical conditions. According to studies, lion's mane mushrooms are good for mood, memory, and cognitive function in addition to having neuroprotective, anti-inflammatory, and antioxidant properties.

Culturally speaking, Asian cuisine and culinary traditions place a great emphasis on Lion's Mane mushrooms, which are revered as a representation of vigor, longevity, and wisdom. In addition to being used in celebratory foods for special occasions and festivities, they are a common ingredient in many traditional recipes, such as soups, stir-fries, hot pots, and medicinal teas. Additionally, lion's mane mushrooms are employed in herbal medicines and traditional medicine preparations, which are said to assist general well-being, improve cognitive function, and support brain health. Lion's Mane mushrooms are used in soups, stir-fries, and medicinal tonics in China, but they are also frequently served in hot pot dishes and as a topping for rice and noodles in Japan.

To sum up, lion's mane mushrooms are a special kind of mushrooms that are appreciated for their unusual look, exceptional health advantages, and adaptability in the kitchen. In addition to their excellent flavor and texture, they are grown and eaten worldwide for their cultural value, potential medical benefits, and wonderful texture.

Lion's Mane mushrooms have a rich history, a varied flavor profile, and a multitude of health advantages that make them a valued ingredient in cuisines and civilizations worldwide. They also encourage creativity in the kitchen.

Reishi (Ganoderma lucidum)

Reishi mushroom, or Ganoderma lucidum, is a highly esteemed and revered species of mushroom valued for its remarkable beauty, rich cultural heritage, and powerful medical effects. Reishi also referred to as Lingzhi in China and Mannentake in Japan, has been utilized for ages in traditional Asian medicine due to its supposed medicinal and physiological properties. To shed light on the relevance of Reishi mushrooms in the realm of fungi, we shall examine their traits, habitat, cultivation techniques, nutritional profile, therapeutic qualities, culinary applications, cultural meaning, and current research in this extensive section.

Large, fan-shaped caps that are usually reddish-brown in color and have a glossy, varnished look are the distinguishing features of reishi mushrooms. When the caps are young, they are shiny and smooth; as they age, they are more woodsy and textured and frequently taste a little bitter. Spores are released for reproduction through microscopic, tightly spaced holes on the undersides of the caps. Reishi mushrooms are usually found in temperate regions of the world, such as Asia, North America, and Europe, growing on decaying hardwood trees, logs, or stumps. They are typically found in hilly areas, woods, and woodlands that have an abundance of organic matter and moisture.

Reishi mushroom cultivation has been more well-known in recent years as people's awareness of the mushrooms' possible medicinal and health advantages has grown. In contrast to numerous other types of mushrooms that are grown on materials like grain or sawdust, Reishi mushrooms are usually grown on hardwood logs or blocks using a process called "forest cultivation" or "log cultivation." To encourage mycelial growth and fruiting, the logs or blocks are inoculated with Reishi mushroom spawn, which is a substrate loaded with mycelium. They are then incubated in a humid, shady setting. Reishi mushrooms start to form after the mycelium has completely colonized the substrate. Eventually, they mature into giant, fan-shaped adult mushrooms.

Reishi mushrooms can also be grown using alternate techniques such as sawdust bag, bottle, jar cultivation, and log cultivation. Reishi mushroom spawn is added to sterilized bags, bottles, or jars of substrate, and the mixture is then incubated in a controlled atmosphere until the mushrooms are ready to be harvested. Due to the increased flexibility and control over growing circumstances provided by these cultivation techniques, Reishi mushrooms can be grown year-round, regardless of seasonal fluctuations.

Since ancient times, traditional Asian medical systems, including Traditional Chinese Medicine (TCM) and Japanese Kampo, have utilized reishi mushrooms, which are highly prized for their possible therapeutic qualities. They are used to treat a range of illnesses, such as respiratory infections, digestive issues, and exhaustion, and are thought to have tonic, adaptogenic, and immune-modulating qualities. Reishi mushrooms are also believed to enhance general health and wellbeing, encouraging vigor, longevity, and resistance to illness and stress. Numerous of these traditional applications have been validated by contemporary scientific study, which shows the medicinal potential of reishi mushrooms in preventing and treating a range of medical disorders.

Research has indicated that Reishi mushrooms are rich in polysaccharides, triterpenoids, sterols, and antioxidants, among other bioactive substances that support its therapeutic qualities. These substances have been demonstrated to positively impact liver function, cardiovascular health, and cognitive function in addition to immunomodulatory, anti-inflammatory, antioxidant, antiviral, and anticancer properties. To add to their overall nutritional worth and health advantages, reishi mushrooms are also rich in vitamins, minerals, and other elements, such as potassium, calcium, magnesium, zinc, and vitamins B and D.

Reishi mushrooms are utilized in cooking, especially in traditional Asian cuisine, in addition to their therapeutic uses. Reishi mushrooms are used to manufacture teas, tinctures, extracts, and supplements that are taken for their possible health advantages, even though they are not usually ingested for their flavor or texture. In China and Japan, reishi mushroom tea is especially well-liked because it is thought to enhance lifespan, health, and spiritual well-being. Because of their tough, woody texture, reishi mushrooms can also be used in soups, stews, broths, and stir-fries, though they are usually taken out before serving.

Reishi mushrooms are revered as a symbol of longevity, immortality, and spiritual enlightenment in Asian folklore and mythology, which gives them a unique cultural significance. For millennia, reishi mushrooms have been regarded as a sacred and ethereal fungus, endowed with magical and supernatural properties according to a variety of traditions and folklore. Reishi mushrooms are often utilized as motifs in decorative arts like pottery, textiles, and paintings. They are also regularly portrayed as symbols of health, prosperity, and harmony in Chinese traditional art and literature.

In summary, reishi mushrooms are a highly respected and cherished type of fungus that are prized for their unique look, rich cultural past, and powerful medical qualities. They have been revered for their ability to support health, vigor, and longevity for generations. They have been utilized for centuries in traditional Asian medicine due to their supposed therapeutic properties and health benefits. Reishi mushrooms continue to awe and inspire veneration among mushroom aficionados and health seekers worldwide because of their complicated biochemistry, nutritional richness, and cultural importance.

Truffles (Tuber spp.)

The genus Tuber contains truffles, which are among the most highly valued and sought-after fungi in the culinary industry. Because of their powerful flavor, unique perfume, and scarcity, these mysterious and aromatic mushrooms have long piqued the interest of chefs, food connoisseurs, and foragers. In many different cuisines worldwide, truffles are regarded as a delicacy and highly valued for their culinary qualities. This in-depth study will examine the traits, environment, production techniques, culinary applications, cultural relevance, and economic significance of truffles, illuminating their attraction and significance within the realm of fungi.

As ectomycorrhizal fungi, truffles coexist symbiotically with the roots of several tree species, such as poplar, oak, hazel, and beech. They usually develop underground in conjunction with the roots of their host trees in temperate and Mediterranean regions with calcareous soils. In exchange for carbohydrates and other necessary nutrients, truffles and these trees have a symbiotic interaction in which the truffles trade water and nutrients. For the truffles and their host trees to survive and thrive, there must be a mycorrhizal relationship.

The unique scent of truffles is what sets them apart; it's commonly described as earthy, musky, spicy, and smelling slightly of garlic, nuts, and spices. When fungi release volatile organic chemicals into the air, animals—especially dogs and pigs—that are used to seek truffles in the wild can smell them and produce the scent associated with truffles. The knobby, uneven form and rough, warty surface of truffles aid in moisture retention and spore protection. Depending on the type and maturity of the fungus, truffles can range in color from black to white to different tones of brown.

Because of their rich flavor and aromatic characteristics, which enhance a variety of cuisines, truffles are highly valued. In gourmet cooking, they are frequently used as a garnish or flavoring ingredient. They add their unique flavor and perfume to dishes like pasta, risotto, eggs, salads, and more by shaving or grating them. Additionally, truffles are used to infuse oils, vinegars, butters, and sauces, giving the resulting dish more depth and richness. Truffles are valued for their possible health advantages in addition to their culinary usage. It is thought that they have anti-inflammatory, immune-stimulating, and antioxidant qualities.

The usage of truffles in cuisine dates back thousands of years in many parts of the world. The ancient Greeks and Romans considered truffles to be aphrodisiacs and connected them to fertility and plenty, which is why they were highly valued. In medieval Europe, truffles held great significance as a symbol of affluence and prosperity. They were frequently served at lavish feasts and banquets attended by aristocrats and aristocracy. Because of their rich flavor and culinary adaptability, truffles are still prized by chefs and food fans as a sign of wealth and indulgence in modern times.

Because of the intricacy of their life cycle and habitat needs, truffle cultivation is renowned for being challenging and has long defied successful commercialization. Truffles require specific environmental conditions, host trees, and mycorrhizal relationships to survive, unlike many other mushroom species that can be cultivated using standardized procedures and substrates. There has yet to be much success in artificially cultivating truffles using inoculated tree seedlings and controlled surroundings because the fungi frequently do not form fruiting bodies or truffles under artificial conditions.

Because of this, truffles are mainly collected by foragers and truffle hunters from their natural habitat. These individuals identify and gather these valuable fungi using their knowledge of the local ecosystems, soil types, and weather patterns. Many places have a long-standing tradition of truffle hunting when foragers use pigs or trained dogs to detect the unique scent of truffles buried beneath the earth. The act of hunting truffles is frequently a private and discreet one, with foragers guarding their hunting areas and only disclosing their hunting spots to reliable allies.

Harvesting truffles is a labor-intensive operation that needs persistence, skill, and patience. Once found, a truffle is delicately dug up with a little shovel or trowel, being cautious not to break the fragile fungus. Since truffles don't keep getting better after they're picked, it's important to gather them while they're at their ripest for the best flavor and aroma. Only the best specimens of truffles are brought to market after they are meticulously cleaned and sifted after harvest.

Around the world, truffles are highly valued and fetch high prices at upscale stores and dining establishments. The most expensive and highly sought-after truffles are the white truffles (Tuber magnatum) from Piedmont, Italy, and the black truffles (Tuber melanosporum) from the Perigord area of France. Said to represent the height of culinary perfection, these truffles are used to make some of the world's most opulent and sumptuous dishes. Other countries where truffles are harvested include Spain, Croatia, Australia, and the United States. These countries value truffles for their distinctive flavors and fragrances.

Truffles are prized for their culinary purposes as well as their possible medical and health advantages. They are utilized in traditional medical systems like Traditional Chinese Medicine (TCM) and Ayurveda for their alleged health advantages since they are said to have anti-inflammatory, immune-boosting, and antioxidant qualities. Numerous of these traditional applications have also been validated by contemporary scientific study, which shows the medicinal potential of truffles in the prevention and treatment of a range of medical disorders.

In conclusion, because of their powerful flavor, unique perfume, and scarcity, truffles are among the most highly sought-after and treasured fungus in the culinary world. They are regarded as a sign of luxury and indulgence and have been used for a very long time in culinary traditions all across the globe. Truffles continue to awe and venerate chefs, food fans, and foragers alike with their exquisite flavor and culinary diversity despite the difficulties associated with cultivation and harvesting.

Lesser-Known Varieties

Thousands of kinds of fungi exist in this enormous and varied world, just waiting to Be explored and enjoyed. Many lesser-known mushroom kinds are just as fascinating and worthy of attention, even though some popular varieties like button mushrooms, shiitake, and portobello are also commonly produced. These less well-known kinds come in many forms, dimensions, hues, and tastes, each with unique qualities and applications in cooking. In this sentence, we will examine several of these lesser-known mushroom kinds in-depth, providing information on their unique characteristics, habitat, cultivation techniques, culinary applications, and possible health advantages.

Maitake mushroom (Grifola frondosa), also referred to as ""Dancing mushroom" or "hen of the woods" is one such uncommon variety. Maitake mushrooms are native to North America, Europe, and Asia. In forested settings, they grow in clusters near the bases of trees, especially oak trees. Their overlapping, fan-shaped caps, and unique aroma—often described as earthy, savory, and somewhat spicy—are what define them. Because of their deep, umami flavor and firm, meaty texture, maitake mushrooms are a common addition to savory recipes like stir-fries and soups. They are prized for their possible health advantages as well and are thought to possess anti-inflammatory, anti-cancer, and immune-boosting qualities.

The chanterelle mushroom (Cantharellus cibarius), which is valued for its delicate flavor, golden color, and unique trumpet-like shape, is another less well-known type. Around the world, chanterelle mushrooms grow in symbiotic relationships with various tree species, such as oak, beech, and pine, in temperate woods. Their smooth, vase-shaped crowns and wavy, ridged undersides, which resemble trumpet folds, are what distinguish them. The solid, meaty texture of chanterelle mushrooms holds up nicely when cooked, and they have a fruity and slightly peppery flavor. They are frequently used as a garnish or topper for pasta, risotto, and other foods after being sautéed, roasted, or grilled.

The lesser-known lobster mushroom (Hypomyces lactifluorum) is highly valued for both its flavor, akin to seafood and its vivid color. The lobster mushroom, despite its name, is actually a parasitic fungus that infects other kinds of mushrooms, usually those in the Lactarius or Russula genera. The host mushroom is changed by the parasitic fungus into a dense, meaty mass that resembles a lobster and has a vivid orange-red color. Lobster mushrooms are a common addition to vegetarian and vegan cuisine because of their mild, somewhat sweet flavor that is reminiscent of shellfish. They are frequently used to soups, stews, and risottos to enhance the taste and color of the food.

The lion's mane mushroom, or Hericium erinaceus, is a distinctive and stunning variation distinguished by its mild flavor akin to seafood and long, cascading spines. Native to Asia, Europe, and North America are lion's mane mushrooms. They grow in enormous, globe-shaped clusters with characteristic white, shaggy spines on rotting hardwood trees. Because of its soft, meaty texture and subtle, seafood-like flavor, lion's mane mushrooms are a common addition to vegetarian and vegan cooking. They are frequently used in seafood dishes in place of crab or lobster and are sautéed, roasted, or grilled.

The delicate, slender kind of enoki mushroom (Flammulina velutipes) is highly valued for its mild flavor and crunchy texture. Enoki mushrooms are native to East

Asia. They grow in clusters on rotting hardwood trees, where they develop small button-like caps and long, pencil-thin stalks. Enoki mushrooms hold up well in cooking and have a crisp texture with a little fruity flavor. They are frequently used to soups, salads, and stir-fries to give the food more flavor and texture. Enoki mushrooms are prized for their possible health advantages and are thought to have anti-inflammatory and immune-stimulating qualities.

An adaptable and commonly cultivated type, oyster mushrooms (Pleurotus ostreatus) are prized for their delicate flavor and soft texture. Oyster mushrooms are native to temperate regions of the world. They grow in enormous, shelf-like clusters with characteristic fan-shaped caps on rotting wood. Oyster mushrooms are a common component in many different recipes because of their soft, meaty texture and mild, somewhat sweet flavor. They are frequently used in soups, stews, pasta dishes, and risotto after being sautéed, stir-fried, or grilled. Additionally prized for their possible health advantages, oyster mushrooms are thought to offer anti-inflammatory and anti-cholesterol effects.

Morel mushrooms (Morchella spp.) are a highly sought-after and difficult-to-find type of mushroom distinguished by its unique look and flavor—a rich, nutty taste. Morel mushrooms are found in woods, woodlands, and grasslands in temperate parts of North America, Europe, and Asia. They bloom in the spring following the first rains. The hollow, spongy innards and conical, honeycomb-like tops of morel mushrooms are their distinguishing features. They are a common component in gourmet cooking because of their solid, meaty texture and rich, nutty flavor. Morel mushrooms are frequently used as a garnish or topping for pasta, risotto, and other meals after being sautéed, roasted, or grilled.

In summary, there are a plethora of lesser-known mushroom types in the world of fungus, each with distinct qualities, tastes, and culinary applications. These lesser-known kinds offer many culinary options and possible health benefits, from the delicate, seafood-like flavor of lion's mane mushrooms to the earthy, savory flavor of maitake mushrooms. Through investigation and experimentation with these varied types of mushrooms, cooks, foodies, and foragers can uncover an array of tastes and textures that enhance and complicate their culinary creations.

CHAPTER IV

Harvesting and Preservation

Knowing When to Harvest

A critical ability for producers, foragers, and mushroom enthusiasts alike is knowing when to harvest mushrooms. When mushrooms are harvested at the correct moment, the fungus and its surrounding ecology are kept healthy, and the mushrooms have the best possible flavor, texture, and nutritional value. This extensive section will examine the variables that affect the timing of the mushroom harvest, the indicators that the harvest is ready, and the most effective methods for harvesting different kinds of mushrooms.

The kind of mushroom, the growth stage, and the surrounding conditions all affect when to harvest mushrooms. While some mushrooms, like oyster and shiitake, can be picked year-round in controlled circumstances, others, like chanterelles and morels, fruit in the spring following the first rains. Determining the ideal time for harvesting requires an understanding of the life cycle and development characteristics of various mushroom species.

The fruiting body's maturity is a crucial feature to take into account when scheduling the mushroom harvest. As they grow, mushrooms go through several developmental stages, from the first primordia to the expansion and fruiting body maturation. Mushrooms are at their most flavorful and nutritious when harvested at the proper time of development. For instance, adult mushrooms may be softer and have a stronger flavor than young mushrooms, which often have a harder texture and a milder flavor.

The development of the fruiting body is not the only aspect that affects when to harvest mushrooms; temperature, humidity, and rainfall are also important considerations. Numerous types of mushrooms bear fruit in reaction to particular environmental cues, including variations in humidity or temperature, which cause primordia to develop and fruiting to begin. By monitoring these environmental variables, mushroom producers and foragers may predict when mushrooms are likely to fruit and schedule their harvest appropriately.

The impact of mushroom harvesting on the health of the fungus and its surrounding ecology is an essential factor to take into account when choosing when to harvest mushrooms. Harvesting mushrooms carelessly or before they've had a chance to release their spores might upset the ecosystem's natural equilibrium and decrease the amount of mushrooms that are available for future generations. To maintain the health of the fungus and its ecosystem, it is imperative to harvest mushrooms in an ethical and sustainable manner, leaving behind enough mushrooms for them to mature and release their spores.

So, how can you determine when it's time to pick mushrooms? The maturity and readiness for harvesting of mushrooms can be determined by a number of indicators. The fruiting body's size and appearance are among the most noticeable indicators. Immature mushrooms can still be tiny and developing, whereas mature mushrooms are usually completely grown and have reached their maximum size. The mushroom's texture and color might also reveal whether or not it's ready to be harvested. Mature mushrooms tend to be tougher and have more vibrant colors than juvenile mushrooms.

The state of the mushroom's gills and cap is a crucial sign of whether it's ready for harvest. Mushrooms that have reached maturity may see their caps flatten or even curl upward, revealing more pronounced gills. As the mushroom ages, its texture may also alter, becoming smoother and more consistent in the gills and cap. Foragers and producers can use these variations in the cap and gill texture and appearance to determine when mushrooms are ready to be harvested.

When they are ready to be harvested, mushrooms occasionally release spores or release unique smells. When chanterelle mushrooms are ready to be harvested, they can have a perfume that is fruity or apricot-like. Still, morel mushrooms are known to have a unique earthy, nutty aroma. Furthermore, when they are grown and ready to be harvested, some mushroom species, particularly puffballs and puffball-like fungi, may emit clouds of spores. Foragers and producers can use these signs and indicators to help them determine when mushrooms are at their best flavor and ready for harvesting.

When mushrooms are considered ready to be harvested, it is crucial to do so with caution and responsibility in order to prevent further harm to the fungus and its natural environment. Using sharp knives or scissors to cut the mushrooms at the base of the stem is essential when harvesting mushrooms in the wild. Take cautious not to harm the mycelium or the nearby plants. It's also critical to harvest mushrooms carefully, allowing enough time for the fungi to mature and release their spores, as the fungus and its ecology need to survive.

It's crucial to harvest cultivated mushrooms, such as shiitake or oyster mushrooms, at the peak of their maturity but before the caps start to open up or flatten. This helps to contain pests and illnesses in the growing environment and guarantees that the mushrooms are at the height of their flavor and nutritional content. It is also imperative to harvest mushrooms with care and gentleness to preserve their delicate fruiting bodies and ensure a consistent harvest throughout the growing season.

In conclusion, producers, foragers, and mushroom enthusiasts all agree that understanding when to harvest mushrooms is an essential skill. By knowing the variables that affect the timing of the harvest and becoming adept at spotting the harvest-ready indicators, people can ensure that they harvest mushrooms at their best flavor, texture, and nutritional value. By collecting mushrooms ethically and sustainably, we may contribute to maintaining the health of the fungus and its surrounding habitat for the enjoyment of future generations.

Harvesting Techniques

Efficient harvesting methods are essential for the successful collection of mushrooms for scientific, gastronomic, or medicinal purposes. To guarantee a plentiful and sustainable harvest while maintaining the health of the fungus and its surrounding ecology, it is vital to comprehend the appropriate techniques for mushroom harvesting. This extensive section will examine the several methods of harvesting that mushroom producers, foragers, and hobbyists employ, such as sustainable harvesting methods, wild harvesting methods, and cultivated methods.

The act of collecting mushrooms from their native habitat in forests, woodlands, grasslands, and other wild ecosystems is known as wild harvesting or foraging. To find and gather mushrooms in the wild, foragers rely on their understanding of the species, habitat preferences, and seasonal variations of local mushrooms. A sustainable harvest depends on meticulous attention to detail and respect for the environment, even if wild harvesting can be an exciting and fulfilling activity. In addition to being knowledgeable of the laws and rules controlling wild gathering in their area, foragers need to be proficient in precisely identifying mushrooms in order to prevent picking toxic or unfit species.

Sustainable harvesting techniques are crucial when collecting mushrooms in the wild to reduce the influence on the fungus and its surrounding ecology. Only fully grown mushrooms should be collected by foragers; young mushrooms should be allowed to ripen and release their spores. In order to prevent harming the fragile fruiting bodies and to cause the least amount of disturbance to the nearby plants and soil, it is equally crucial to carefully and gently harvest mushrooms. In order to avoid disturbing the mycelium or the surrounding ecosystem, foragers should slice the mushrooms at the stem's base with scissors or sharp knives.

Harvesting mushrooms that have been produced and developed in controlled environments—such as indoor grow rooms, greenhouses, or mushroom farms—is referred to as "cultivated harvesting." Typically, substrate materials like sawdust, straw, compost, or grain are used to grow cultivated mushrooms because they supply the nutrients and moisture that the mushrooms require to grow. To achieve ideal fruiting and yield, harvesting grown mushrooms necessitates careful monitoring of growing conditions, including temperature, humidity, and light levels. In order to harvest mushrooms at the height of their flavor and nutritional value, growers must also be able to spot the telltale signals of harvest readiness.

To avoid contamination and spoiling, it's crucial to harvest grown mushrooms using the right hygiene and sanitation techniques. Before handling mushrooms, growers should properly wash their hands. They should also harvest and handle the mushrooms using sterile equipment. Additionally, to guarantee a high-quality harvest and prevent harm to the fragile fruiting bodies, mushroom harvesting must be done gently and carefully. Harvesting mushrooms involves cutting them at the base of the stem with sharp knives or scissors, taking care not to harm the substrate or mycelium surrounding it.

Sustainable harvesting practices are required to preserve the long-term wellbeing and vigor of neighboring ecosystems as well as mushroom populations. Harvesting mushrooms sustainably entails taking care of them so that the fungus can proliferate and regenerate, providing a steady supply of mushrooms for coming generations. This could entail limiting disturbance to the nearby flora and soil, avoiding overharvesting in vulnerable environments, and leaving behind enough mushrooms to develop and release their spores. Monitoring mushroom populations and habitats closely is also necessary for sustainable harvesting to make sure that harvesting methods do not harm the fungus or its ecology.

Specialized harvesting techniques are employed for particular mushroom species or growth conditions, in addition to wild and cultivated harvesting methods. For instance, truffle hunting entails employing pigs or dogs that have been trained to detect the elusive and highly valued truffles that are hidden underneath. To find and gather these valuable mushrooms, which are frequently found in isolated and difficult-to-access areas, truffle hunters must rely on their understanding of the regional ecosystems, soil types, and weather patterns. Using mushroom rakes or hooks to carefully remove mushrooms from the forest floor without uprooting other plants or soil is another specialist mushroom harvesting method.

In conclusion, whether collecting mushrooms in the wild or under cultivation, effective harvesting methods are essential. Foragers, growers, and mushroom enthusiasts may guarantee a plentiful and sustainable harvest while maintaining the health of the fungus and its surrounding ecosystem by learning the correct techniques for harvesting mushrooms and putting sustainable harvesting practices into practice. A successful and pleasurable mushroom harvest depends on using the right harvesting techniques, whether you're gathering mushrooms in your backyard, on a mushroom farm, or in the forest.

Storing Fresh Mushrooms

For fresh mushrooms to retain their nutritional value, flavor, and quality for as long as possible, proper storage is necessary. When it comes time to utilize mushrooms in your favorite recipes, knowing how to store them properly will prolong their shelf life, whether you've bought them from a shop or foraged them from the wild. We will examine several techniques and recommended practices for preserving fresh mushrooms in order to enhance their flavor and freshness in this extensive section.

First and foremost, it's critical to realize that, in contrast to other fruits and vegetables, mushrooms are highly perishable and have a short shelf life. Because of their high moisture content and fragile texture, they are easily spoiled; therefore, handling and to prevent them from spoiling too quickly, proper storage is crucial. Moisture is one of the most crucial things to take into account while preserving fresh mushrooms. Mushrooms that have too much moisture may become sticky or mushy, while those that have too little moisture may dry out and shrivel.

Fresh mushrooms are best kept in the refrigerator in a paper bag or breathable container. Mushrooms should not be kept in plastic bags or containers as this might retain moisture and encourage the growth of germs and mold. To absorb any extra moisture, move the mushrooms to a paper bag or lightly wrap them in a paper towel. The bag or wrapped mushrooms are better kept in your refrigerator's vegetable crisper drawer, which is also a little bit more stable and colder.

If you bought mushrooms wrapped in plastic wrap or in a plastic container, it's preferable to remove them from their original packaging before keeping them. As mentioned above, move the mushrooms to a paper bag or breathable container to promote airflow and avoid moisture accumulation. If the mushrooms have already been chopped or sliced, keep them separated from one another by storing them in a shallow container covered with paper towels to absorb excess moisture.

Utilizing mushrooms as soon as possible after refrigerating them is crucial to preserving their freshness and flavor. For best freshness, mushrooms should be consumed two to three days after harvesting or purchase. There are a few more techniques you can try to increase the shelf life of mushrooms if you need to preserve them for longer periods of time.

Keeping fresh mushrooms in a glass jar with water inside is a common way to extend their shelf life. To accomplish this, trim the mushroom stems and put them in a clean glass jar with enough water to cover them. After covering the jar with plastic wrap or a lid, place the jar in the refrigerator. To keep the water fresh and prevent the mushrooms from being slimy or discolored, change the water every day or two.

Blanching the mushrooms before storing them is another way to increase their shelf life. To stop the cooking process, blanching entails quickly submerging the mushrooms in boiling water and then cooling them down with ice water. Blanching can increase the shelf life of mushrooms by several days and aid in the destruction of any bacteria or mold spores on their surface. The mushrooms should be completely drained and dried with paper towels after blanching before being put in the fridge.

Consider freezing extra mushrooms if you won't be using them all in a few days. This will allow them to stay fresher for longer. You may enjoy mushrooms in your favorite dishes all year long by freezing them, which is a practical way to keep them fresh and flavorful for several months. Clean and cut the mushrooms into suitable pieces prior to freezing them in a single layer on a parchment paper-lined baking sheet. After the mushrooms are frozen firm, move them Transfer the baked goods to a freezer-safe container or resealable plastic bag for safekeeping. Frozen mushrooms can be added to stir fries, soups, stews, and other cooked meals right out of the freezer without needing to thaw.

You can attempt a few other strategies in addition to these ones to extend the fresh mushroom's shelf life. Save washing mushrooms for when you're ready to use them, as too much moisture might speed up their deterioration. Instead, use a damp paper towel or gentle Before storing them, brush them to get rid of any dirt or debris. Store mushrooms away from strong-smelling items like garlic and onions since they absorb scents easily. Lastly, to avoid contaminating other meals, throw away the mushrooms right away if you see any indications of deterioration, such as mildew, slime, or disagreeable smells.

In conclusion, fresh mushrooms must be stored properly to preserve their flavor, freshness, and nutritional content. You can increase the shelf life of fresh mushrooms and use them in your favorite recipes for longer by adhering to these guidelines and best practices. To keep mushrooms fresh and delicious, store them in the pantry, freezer, or refrigerator, but make sure they are dry, well-ventilated, and kept away from strong-smelling foods. You may always savor the delicious flavor and adaptability of fresh mushrooms by following the proper preservation methods.

Drying, Freezing, and Canning Methods

The three most prevalent methods to preserve mushrooms to increase their shelf life and enjoy them all year round are drying, freezing, and canning. Every method has its own advantages and things to keep in mind, so fans of mushrooms can select the best preservation method for their needs based on equipment availability, personal preferences, and storage space. The processes involved, success strategies, and suggested applications for preserved mushrooms will all be covered in this extensive section as we examine the drying, freezing, and canning techniques for mushroom preservation.

With a history spanning centuries, drying is among the most established and conventional techniques for preserving mushrooms. By removing moisture, drying preserves the flavor and nutritional content of the mushrooms while preventing the formation of mold and germs. Prior to drying mushrooms, give them a complete cleaning to remove any debris or filth. Slice the mushrooms into consistent pieces and trim the stems to promote even drying. Make sure the sliced mushrooms are not in contact with one another when you arrange them in a single layer on a baking sheet or dehydrator tray. After the mushrooms have dried completely, place the baking sheet or dehydrator tray in a well-ventilated area with good airflow, like next to a window or beneath a ceiling fan. The drying process could take a few hours or many days, depending on the size and moisture content of the mushrooms

When completely dried, the mushrooms should be crisp and leathery, with no liquid left on them. They should be kept out of direct sunlight in a cold, dark place, airtight container, or resealable plastic bag. To rehydrate dried mushrooms, immerse them in hot water for 15 to 20 minutes or until they become tender and supple. Rehydrated mushrooms give umami richness and depth of flavor to various foods, such as stir-fries, stews, soups, and sauces.

Another well-liked technique for preserving mushrooms is freezing, which provides a practical and efficient means of increasing their shelf life without sacrificing flavor or texture. Prior to freezing mushrooms, give them a thorough cleaning and cut off any stiff stems or woody portions. Depending on your intended usage and personal preference, you can either slice the mushrooms into uniform pieces or leave them whole. The optional step of blanching can aid in maintaining the texture and color of the mushrooms when they are frozen. Place the mushrooms in a pot of boiling water to blanch them. To stop the cooking process, quickly move the mushrooms to a bowl of ice water after they have been boiling for one or two minutes. Before freezing, ensure the mushrooms are well drained and dried with paper towels.

After the mushrooms are ready in a single layer on a baking sheet covered with parchment paper., and freeze for as long as needed. For long-term storage, move the frozen mushrooms to an airtight container or resealable plastic bag. Without having to thaw, frozen mushrooms can be utilized straight out of the freezer into stir-fries, soups, stews, and other cooked meals. When it comes to preserving mushrooms for cooking or using them in recipes where texture isn't as crucial, including sauces, soups, and casseroles, freezing is a great choice.

Although canning requires more work than freezing or refrigeration, it has the benefit of shelf-stable storage for mushrooms. In order to produce a vacuum seal and stop the mushrooms from spoiling, canning entails placing them into sterilized glass jars and treating them in a boiling water bath or pressure canner. Prior to canning mushrooms, give them a thorough cleaning and clip off any tough stems or blemishes. Depending on your intended usage and personal preference, you can either slice the mushrooms into uniform pieces or leave them whole.

CHAPTER V

Culinary Delights

Cooking Techniques and Tips

Mushroom cooking is an art form that demands creativity, attention to detail, and knowledge of the distinctive qualities of various mushroom types. Mushrooms have earthy aromas and delicate textures that can be enhanced by learning several cooking techniques, such as sautéing, grilling, roasting, or simmering. This can make mushrooms stand out as a star element in any recipe. This extensive section will cover a wide range of mushroom preparation methods, from simple sautéing to more complex approaches like filled mushrooms and mushroom risotto.

One of the most well-liked and adaptable methods for cooking mushrooms is sautéing, which lets you cook them fast to a soft perfection while bringing out their inherent tastes. First, slice the mushrooms into uniform pieces after giving them a good cleaning. Place a tiny quantity of oil or Melt the butter in a skillet or frying pan over medium-high heat. Don't overcrowd the pan when the oil is heated; instead, put the sliced mushrooms in a single layer. Let the mushrooms cook for a few minutes without stirring until they begin to release moisture and turn brown. Stir them once in a while to make sure they cook evenly. After the mushrooms are soft and golden brown, Season to taste with salt, pepper, and any other herbs or spices.

Another well-liked method of preparing mushrooms is grilling, which produces a deliciously earthy flavor that blends in perfectly with the smokey, charred flavor. To grill mushrooms, first give them a good cleaning and coat them with marinade or olive oil to keep them from sticking and to add taste. After preheating the grill to medium-high temperature, put the mushrooms straight onto the grates. The mushrooms should be soft and gently browned after a few minutes of cooking on each side, turning them from time to time. You can have grilled mushrooms as a side dish, top burgers and pizzas, or add them to salads and sandwiches.

Roasting mushrooms brings out their inherent sweetness and rich flavor. It's a simple yet effective cooking method. First, prepare the mushrooms by giving them a thorough cleaning and chopping them into little pieces. Spread the mushrooms in a single layer on a baking sheet covered with parchment paper after tossing them with olive oil, salt, pepper, and any additional herbs or seasonings you like. Preheat the oven to 400°F (200°C). Roast the mushrooms for 15 to 20 minutes, tossing periodically, or until they are soft and browned. Roasted mushrooms can be topped with pizza and bruschetta, eaten as a side dish, or added to pasta meals or grain bowls.

By using a gradual cooking method called simmering, mushrooms are able to absorb the characteristics of the liquid they are cooked in, which results in a rich, delicious broth or sauce and tender, fragrant mushrooms. First, slice the mushrooms into uniform pieces after giving them a good cleaning. Add a small quantity of butter or oil to a big saucepan or Dutch oven and heat it over medium heat. The mushrooms should be added to the pot with the oil already heated and cooked until they begin to release moisture and turn a light brown. Add any additional ingredients you choose, like broth, onions, garlic, or herbs, and cook the mushrooms until they are soft and flavorful. Savory pies and tarts can be filled with sautéed mushrooms, or they can be served as a stand-alone dish.

Beyond these fundamental methods of preparation, there are a gazillion ways to experiment in the kitchen when it comes to mushrooms. For instance, you may make vegetarian meals like mushroom stir-fries, tacos, and burgers by substituting mushrooms for the meat. Moreover, you may stuff mushrooms with a range of mixtures—including cheese, breadcrumbs, herbs, and spices—and bake them until they're bubbling and brown. Making mushroom risotto, a creamy, cozy meal that highlights the rich, earthy flavor of mushrooms in every bite, is another well-liked cooking method.

It is crucial to select the appropriate type of mushrooms for the dish you are preparing when cooking with them. It's crucial to try with a variety of mushrooms to find your favorite kind because they all have various flavors, textures, and culinary uses. With their distinct flavor profiles and culinary applications, button, cremini, shiitake, oyster, and portobello mushrooms are a few of the often used mushroom types in cuisine.

To guarantee that the mushrooms are cooked to perfection, it's also critical to monitor the cooking temperature and duration when working with mushrooms. Undercooking mushrooms can produce a harsh, chewy texture while overcooking them can make them mushy and flavorless. It's preferable to cook mushrooms over medium-high heat for a little period of time, stirring from time to time, until they become soft and brown. It's recommended to prepare the mushrooms separately and add them to the meal at the end of cooking if you're adding them to a stew or soup to avoid overcooking them.

In conclusion, exploring the rich, earthy flavors and delicate textures of these adaptable fungi through cooking is a satisfying and diverse culinary effort. Whether you're roasting, sautéing, grilling, or simmering,

Being able to cook a wide range of foods will enable you to create satisfying, delicious meals that showcase the unique qualities of mushrooms. You may explore a world of gourmet possibilities and improve your cooking to new levels by experimenting with various mushroom kinds, seasonings, and cooking techniques. So go ahead and use your imagination in the kitchen to make mushrooms the focal point of your next dish!

Mushroom Recipes from Around the World

Around the world, mushrooms are a highly appreciated and adaptable ingredient in cuisines due to their distinct tastes, textures, and healthful properties. Mushrooms are employed in a variety of dishes that highlight their flexibility and versatility in different culinary traditions, from flavorful stir-fries to hearty soups and comforting stews. This extensive section will examine a variety of mushroom recipes from various locales and civilizations, showcasing the various ways that mushrooms are cooked and consumed globally.

Let's begin our culinary exploration in Italy, where Risotto, spaghetti, and pizza are some of the classic recipes that feature mushrooms. Risotto ai Funghi is a traditional Italian mushroom meal consisting of Arborio rice, mushrooms, onions, garlic, white wine, and Parmesan cheese. It's a creamy and satisfying dish. To make Risotto ai Funghi, begin by softly sautéing chopped garlic and onions in olive oil until transparent. Stir the Arborio rice in the oil and heat, stirring regularly, until the rice is lightly browned and coated. Add the chicken or vegetable broth gradually while constantly tossing until the rice is cooked through and creamy. Add the sliced mushrooms and grated Parmesan cheese to the Risotto after cooking them in butter in a separate pan until they turn golden brown. For an added touch of refinement, serve the hot Risotto with chopped parsley and a drizzle of truffle oil.

Next, we travel to France, where we discover Coq au Vin, a traditional mushroom dish that has won over the hearts and palates of foodies everywhere. This filling and aromatic French dish is made with chicken that has been cooked in red wine, along with bacon, onions, mushrooms, and herbs. First, cook the chicken pieces in a big skillet or Dutch oven until they are golden brown all over before making the coq au vin. After taking out and setting aside the chicken, add the chopped onions, garlic, and sliced mushrooms to the pan and sauté them until they become tender. Add the chicken back to the pan with the diced bacon, bay leaves, fresh thyme, and a bottle of dry red wine. Once the chicken is cooked and the flavors have combined, cover the pan and boil the meal gently for around one hour. Serve Coq au Vin hot, with mashed potatoes or crusty bread on the side to mop up the flavorful sauce.

When we journey to Asia, we come across yet another lively and varied food culture that honors mushrooms in a wide range of recipes. Stir-fried mushrooms with veggies, meats, and sauces are a common way to prepare flavorful and filling dishes in Chinese cuisine, such as Stir-fried Mushrooms with Garlic and Bok Choy. To begin preparing this dish, Add a little quantity of oil to a wok or large pan and heat it over high heat. Sliced mushrooms and minced garlic should be added to the pan and stir-fried until the mushrooms are soft and begin to become golden brown. When the greens are smooth and wilted, add more chopped bok choy or other leafy greens to the pan and stir-fry. Serve hot with noodles or steaming rice for a tasty and wholesome dinner. Season with soy sauce, oyster sauce, and a dash of sugar.

Mushrooms are highly appreciated in Japan for their delicate texture and umami-rich flavor; they are frequently used in noodle dishes, soups, and stews. Kinoko Gohan, a straightforward and filling rice meal cooked with mushrooms, soy sauce, and dashi broth, is one well-known Japanese mushroom recipe. Rinse short-grain rice under cold water until the water runs clear, then drain and let soak for around half an hour to prepare Kinoko Gohan. Meanwhile, prepare a variety of mushrooms, including shimeji, enoki, and shiitake, by cleaning and slicing them. After the rice has soaked, drain it and combine it with the sliced mushrooms, soy sauce, mirin, and dashi broth in a skillet or rice cooker. Cook the rice until it's fluffy and soft, following the manufacturer's recommendations. To add more taste and texture, serve hot Kinoko Gohan with sliced green onions and toasted sesame seeds as garnish.

Mushrooms are a common ingredient in many classic Mexican recipes, such as soups, tacos, and quesadillas. They give these foods depth and richness. Rajas with Crema y Champiñones is a traditional Mexican mushroom recipe that combines roasted poblano peppers, onions, mushrooms, and cream to create a tasty and creamy dish. To prepare Rajas with Crema y Champiñones, begin by roasting poblano peppers over an open flame or under the broiler until they are blistered and blackened all over. After the peppers have been roasted, once they're in a covered bowl or plastic bag, steam them for approximately 10 minutes. Then, remove the seeds and stems, after removing the burnt outer layer, cut the peppers into thin strips. In the interim, place sliced onions and mushrooms in a big skillet set over medium heat. After adding the sliced poblano peppers and a liberal portion of Mexican crema, or sour cream, sauté the vegetables until they are tender and lightly browned. After a few minutes of cooking, when the mixture is well cooked and creamy, add some salt, pepper, and lime juice for seasoning. For a tasty and filling dinner, serve hot Rajas with Crema y Champiñones with warm tortillas or rice on the side.

In India, mushrooms are frequently used in vegetarian meals such as Mushroom Masala, a fragrant and spicy curry prepared with tomatoes, onions, and mushrooms, along with a variety of aromatic spices.In a big pan or Dutch oven, heat the oil over medium heat before making the mushroom masala. Add the chopped garlic, ginger, and green chilies and heat for an additional minute or until aromatic. Next, add the diced onions and sauté until they are tender and golden brown. When the tomatoes begin to break down and release their juices, add chopped tomatoes to the pan. Next, add sliced mushrooms and a mixture of ground spices, such as cumin, turmeric, coriander, and garam masala. After the mixture has cooked for a few minutes and the mushrooms are soft and covered in the hot sauce, add a splash of cream or coconut milk for more richness and creaminess. Serve hot Mushroom Masala with naan bread or steaming rice on the side for a filling and aromatic dinner.

In conclusion, because of their distinct flavors, textures, and culinary diversity, mushrooms are a popular and adaptable element in cuisines all over the world. There are many ways to enjoy mushrooms in a wide range of tasty and gratifying recipes, from Mexican Rajas con Crema y Champiñones to Indian Mushroom Masala, Chinese stir-fries to Japanese Kinoko Gohan, and Italian Risotto to French coq au vin. You may find a world of flavor and culinary inspiration that will please your taste buds and nurture your body and spirit by investigating the various culinary traditions that celebrate mushrooms and experimenting with different cooking methods and recipes. So go ahead and use your imagination in the kitchen to create your next culinary marvel, showcasing mushrooms prominently!

Health Benefits of Mushrooms

As varied and abundant as the many kinds of mushrooms themselves are the health advantages of eating them. Mushrooms are a popular addition to meals because of their distinct texture and rich umami flavor. They are also a nutritional powerhouse, full of important vitamins, minerals, and antioxidants. Mushrooms are a great addition to any diet because of their many health advantages, which range from enhancing immune function to supporting heart health and cognitive performance.

The capacity of mushrooms to boost immune system performance and strengthen the body's defenses against illness and infection is one of their most well-known health advantages. Beta-glucans are a form of polysaccharide found in mushrooms that have been demonstrated to increase white blood cell production, which strengthens immunity and is necessary to fight off infections and diseases. Moreover, the body's defense mechanism is supported by antioxidants found in abundance in mushrooms, such as selenium, vitamin C, and vitamin D, which scavenge negative free radicals that cause oxidative damage and inflammation.

Mushrooms have been demonstrated to strengthen immunological function, reduce the chance of heart disease and enhance heart health. According to studies, beta-glucans and sterols, two substances present in mushrooms, have the ability to improve lipid metabolism and lower cholesterol, both of which may lower the risk of heart disease. Potassium, a mineral that supports healthy heart function and blood pressure regulation, is abundant in mushrooms. By including mushrooms in your diet as part of a heart-healthy eating plan, you can lower your chance of developing heart disease and promote cardiovascular health.

In addition, mushrooms are a great source of vital vitamins and minerals that are critical for good health and wellbeing in general. For instance, one of the few naturally occurring dietary sources of the essential vitamin D foods high in vitamin D, which is essential. Vitamin D is essential for powerful bones, a strong immune system, and steady moods, is found in mushrooms. Since there is often a deficiency of vitamin D, especially in places with limited sunlight, eating mushrooms can help ensure you are getting adequate of this important nutrient. Furthermore, B vitamins, including pantothenic acid, Mushrooms are a great source of niacin and riboflavin, which are essential for healthy neural system function and energy metabolism.

In addition, mushrooms are an excellent option for managing weight and maintaining digestive health because they are low in calories and fat yet high in fiber. Because mushrooms are high in fiber, they can improve weight loss attempts by preventing overeating by promoting feelings of fullness and satiety. Furthermore, by nourishing good gut flora and avoiding constipation and other digestive problems, the soluble fiber in mushrooms helps to control blood sugar levels and support a healthy digestive system.

The ability of mushrooms to maintain cognitive function and guard against age-related cognitive decline is another intriguing feature of these plants. Studies have demonstrated that certain chemicals found in mushrooms, such as erinacines and hericenones, have the ability to increase the brain's synthesis of nerve growth factor (NGF). Age-related decreases in NGF synthesis have been connected to neurological conditions like Parkinson's and Alzheimer's, as well as cognitive decline. NGF is a protein that is essential to the development, survival, and upkeep of nerve cells. Mushrooms may improve brain health and guard against age-related cognitive decline by increasing the synthesis of NGF.

In addition, studies have been conducted on mushrooms' possible anti-cancer effects and their capacity to stop the growth and spread of cancer cells. Studies have indicated that polysaccharides, lectins, and phenolic compounds—compounds with anti-inflammatory, antioxidant, and anti-cancer properties—are present in mushrooms. It has been demonstrated that these substances prevent angiogenesis, the development of new blood arteries that supply tumors, stop the growth of tumors, andcause to experience programmed cell death, or apoptosis, in cancer cells. Although preliminary evidence suggests that eating more mushrooms may help improve the outcomes of cancer therapies cause apoptosis, another name for programmed cell death, in cancerous cells. further studies are needed to completely understand the anti-cancer potential of mushrooms.

Furthermore, it has been demonstrated that mushrooms contain haracteristics that may help reduce inflammation and soothe the signs and symptoms of inflammatory conditions including inflammatory bowel illness, asthma, and arthritis. Compounds found in mushrooms, such as ergothioneine and selenium, have been demonstrated to suppress inflammatory pathways and lower the generation of inflammatory cytokines, which are chemicals that cause tissue damage and chronic inflammation. You may enhance general health and well-being and lessen inflammation by including mushrooms in your diet as part of an anti-inflammatory eating plan.

Mushrooms have also been researched for their ability to elevate mood and lessen anxiety and depressive symptoms. Compounds found in mushrooms, such as vitamin D and selenium, have been demonstrated to control mood and serotonin levels in the brain. This can enhance mood and lessen the signs of anxiety and sadness. Furthermore, ergothioneine and glutathione, two antioxidants connected to mood disorders, are abundant in mushrooms and aid in protecting the brain from inflammatory and oxidative stress. Enhancing mental and emotional health can be achieved through including mushrooms in your diet as part of a well-rounded, nutrient-dense eating plan.

In summary, mushrooms are a nutrient-dense, adaptable food that has a host of health advantages, including boosting heart health, lowering cancer risk, and strengthening immunological system performance. Mushrooms are a great complement to any diet because of their rich umami flavor, distinct texture, and outstanding nutritional profile. They can also be used in various delectable and fulfilling recipes. Mushrooms are a tasty and adaptable food that may enhance your health and wellbeing in a variety of ways. You can use them as a stir-fry element, sauté them in a pan, or stuff them with savory fillings. So embrace the power of mushrooms and enjoy all the health advantages that these unique fungus have to offer!.

CHAPTER VI

Mushroom Foraging

Identifying Wild Edible Mushrooms

The foragers can enjoy the delectable flavors and nutritional advantages of these adaptable fungi while connecting with nature by learning to identify wild edible mushrooms, which is an exciting and satisfying endeavor. But be cautious and mindful of the environment when mushroom misidentification can result in severe sickness or even death. It is possible for anyone to identify and safely gather a wide range of edible wild mushrooms with the correct information, monitoring, and instruction.

Learning the traits of many mushroom families and species is one of the first steps toward identifying edible wild mushrooms. There are several taxonomic categories that include mushrooms, and each has unique characteristics, preferred habitats, and edible qualities. Among the groups of mushrooms that are commonly consumed are the Russulaceae (brittlegills), Boletaceae (boletes), and Agaricaceae (gilled mushrooms). Foragers can become proficient in identifying edible specimens in the wild by studying field guides, participating in mushroom identification seminars, and joining mushroom hunting groups. These activities will teach them to identify the distinctive characteristics of various mushroom species.

It is essential to pay great attention to the area and ecosystem in which wild edible mushrooms flourish when out foraging. Different species of mushrooms enjoy different types of habitats, including grasslands, meadows, urban areas, and even coniferous and deciduous woods. Specific types of trees are ideal for particular kinds of mushrooms to grow in symbiotic relationships with, while other types of mushrooms do well in organic waste that is decomposing, such as leaf litter, rotting wood, or animal dung. Foragers can focus their search and raise their chances of discovering edible mushrooms by paying attention to the trees, plants, and soil conditions in the area.

Analyzing the morphological traits of the mushroom, such as its cap, gills, stem, and spore print, is another crucial step in the identification process. Because edible mushrooms can have a broad variety of sizes, textures, colors, and shapes, it's critical to consider specifics like stem morphology, gill attachment, cap shape, and overall look. Boletes, on the other hand, usually have a cap with a sponge-like pore surface and a thick, fleshy stem, whereas many edible gilled mushrooms have a convex or umbonate cap with free or attached gills and a central or off-center stem. Furthermore, obtaining a spore print— which is as simple as setting a mushroom cap on paper and waiting for it to spew spores—can assist in identifying the particular mushroom and reducing the number of possible species.

While some wild mushrooms are easily identified and safe to consume, identification is crucial for safe harvesting since certain wild mushrooms closely mimic dangerous or lethal species. Toxins found in many poisonous mushrooms can result in severe gastrointestinal distress, damage to the liver or kidneys, neurological symptoms, or even death if consumed. As such, you should always err on the side of caution and avoid eating wild mushrooms unless you are positive about their identity and safety. When in doubt, seek advice from knowledgeable mycologists, mushroom hunters, or local specialists who can confirm the nature of the mushroom and offer safety tips.

When gathering wild edible mushrooms, foragers should take into account sustainable and ethical harvesting methods in addition to accurate identification. Overharvesting can jeopardize delicate species and disturb natural ecological processes, which can have a negative impact on mushroom populations and ecosystems. Consequently, it's critical to responsibly harvest mushrooms, removing only what you need and leaving enough behind to guarantee their continuous development and reproduction. Foragers should also always abide by local laws and regulations controlling the gathering and foraging of mushrooms in order to prevent harming the nearby flora, ecosystems, and fauna.

Starting cautiously and concentrating on a few edible mushroom species that are commonly known and easily identified is one of the best methods to assure safe and successful mushroom foraging. Only then should you expand out to more difficult or obscure types. A few popular edible mushrooms that are suitable for novices are the versatile oyster mushroom (Pleurotus ostreatus), the delicious shiitake mushroom (Lentinula edodes), and the common white button mushroom (Agaricus bisporus). Novice foragers can build confidence in their ability to identify edible mushrooms by becoming familiar with these and other well-known varieties. As they gain experience and knowledge, they can then gradually broaden their repertoire.

It's also critical to understand that mushroom foraging is a lifetime learning process and that even seasoned foragers can gain from continued education, guidance, and enthusiast participation. Participating in citizen science projects, attending forays and workshops, joining mushroom clubs, and interacting with online forums and social media communities are all great ways to meet other mushroom enthusiasts, exchange experiences and knowledge, and keep honing and expanding your identification skills.

To sum up, finding wild edible mushrooms is a pleasant and rewarding activity that provides a special chance to get in touch with nature, discover various ecosystems, and savor the flavor and health advantages of these amazing fungi. Through the acquisition of mushroom identification skills, careful observation of the habitat and surrounding conditions, and the use of moral and sustainable harvesting techniques, foragers can extend their culinary horizons while enjoying the forest's bounty in a safe and responsible manner. In the intriguing realm of wild edible mushrooms, there's always something new to learn and explore, regardless of experience level or level of curiosity.

Safety Precautions and Regulations

Regulations and safety measures should be the top priorities for everyone who harvests or forages mushrooms. While mushroom hunting and growing can be lucrative and fun pursuits, there are risks involved that must be considered, such as the possibility of unintentionally ingesting deadly mushrooms, harm to the ecosystem, and legal repercussions. A safe and happy experience can be ensured by foragers and cultivators by minimizing hazards, protecting themselves and the environment, and learning and following safety procedures and regulations.

Correct identification is one of the most essential safety measures when it comes to mushroom foraging. Since many dangerous species of mushrooms superficially resemble edible ones, misidentifying wild mushrooms can have serious repercussions. As such, it's critical to become well-versed in the traits of both edible and hazardous mushroom species, including appearance, growth patterns, and habitat. When in doubt, it's always better to Never consume a wild mushroom unless foragers are confident in its identify and edible quality. Always err on the side of caution. Enhancing identification abilities and lowering the possibility of unintentional poisoning can be achieved by consulting field guides, going to identification workshops, and getting advice from knowledgeable mycologists or foragers.

Foragers can reduce their impact on mushroom populations and habitats by using ethical and sustainable gathering methods in addition to appropriate identification. Overharvesting can have a negative effect on wild mushroom populations, putting delicate species in danger and upsetting normal ecological processes. In order to ensure that mushrooms continue to grow and reproduce, foragers should gather mushrooms in a responsible manner, taking only what they need and leaving behind enough. Foragers should also always abide by local laws and regulations controlling the gathering and foraging of mushrooms in order to prevent harming the nearby flora, ecosystems, and fauna.

When foraging in natural places, foragers should also be aware of potential threats and hazards to the environment. Risks to the safety and well-being of foragers include exposure to ticks, poison ivy, or other poisonous plants; weather conditions that are unfavorable; and confrontations with wildlife. Wearing adequate clothing and footwear, having a first aid kit, compass, and flashlight on hand, as well as being ready for unexpected weather and emergencies, are therefore imperative. Before heading into the bush, foragers should also familiarize themselves with local emergency contacts and procedures and let someone know where they are and the path they plan to take.

Safety measures are equally vital in mushroom growth to guarantee a good and safe growing experience. In order to stop contamination and the development of dangerous bacteria, fungus, or pests in the ever-increasing environment, proper hygiene and sanitation measures are crucial. To reduce the danger of contamination, cultivators should routinely clean and sterilize tools, equipment, and growing containers in addition to keeping their workplaces tidy and clean. Cultivators should also purchase substrates, growth supplies, and premium mushroom spawn from reliable vendors to guarantee ideal growing conditions and reduce the possibility of contamination or illness.

In addition, growers need to be mindful of the possible risks connected to growing mushrooms, like coming into contact with harmful substances, allergies, or infections. Chemical pesticides, fertilizers, and disinfectants may be employed in some mushroom growing techniques; if not utilized appropriately, these substances could be hazardous to human health and the environment. Thus, when handling and applying chemicals, cultivators should adhere to safety regulations and take the necessary safety precautions. These include donning the proper protective gear, like as goggles, masks, and gloves, and closely reading product instructions and recommended application rates. Furthermore, growers need to be aware of any possible allergies or poisons connected to specific species of mushrooms and take the necessary safety measures to reduce danger and exposure.

Foragers and growers of mushrooms should take safety precautions. Still, they should also be aware of and follow all relevant laws and rules pertaining to the gathering, growing, and selling of mushrooms. Before partaking in these activities, it is imperative should get familiar with local laws and ordinances that govern the collection and production of mushrooms, as they vary by area and jurisdiction. Foraging for mushrooms in public parks or other protected areas may be restricted in certain places, and commercial mushroom harvesting or sales may need permits or licenses in others. In addition to avoiding legal problems, foragers and growers can make sure their operations are carried out responsibly and sustainably by being aware of and abiding by the relevant legislation.

In conclusion, everybody involved in mushroom cultivation or foraging must take safety precautions and regulations into account. A safe and joyful experience can be ensured by foragers and cultivators by minimizing hazards, protecting themselves and the environment, and adhering to ethical harvesting procedures and environmental stewardship. Furthermore, it's imperative to adhere to safety protocols and laws when managing chemicals, machinery, and other possible risks related to mushroom farming. Foragers and growers can reap the many benefits of mushroom hunting and cultivation while reducing risks and encouraging safety and sustainability in their operations by being aware of and following safety procedures and regulations.

Sustainable Foraging Practices

For ecosystems to remain healthy, biodiversity to be preserved, and wild food supplies to be viable over the long term, sustainable foraging techniques are crucial. It's essential to collect in a way that minimizes adverse effects on the environment while fostering the regeneration and resilience of natural ecosystems, whether you're foraging for berries, wild greens, mushrooms, or other edible plants. Foragers can partake in the bountiful offerings of nature and help preserve and manage wild food supplies for future generations by adopting sustainable foraging practices.

Harvesting only what is necessary and leaving behind enough nutrients to enable the ongoing growth and reproduction of wild plants and fungus is one of the core ideas of sustainable foraging. Overharvesting can upset the ecological balance, reduce the number of wild edible plants and fungus, and endanger the existence of delicate species. To maintain the population's health and viability, foragers should harvest wild foods with moderation and restraint, taking just what they can utilize and leaving plenty of adult individuals behind

In order to reduce their influence on delicate ecosystems, foragers should also give preference to gathering non-threatened or invasive species over rare or endangered ones. Harvesting these species might lessen pressure on vulnerable or threatened populations of wild food plants and fungi since they are more plentiful and robust than other species. Foragers can reap the benefits of a sustainable and ethical harvest while safeguarding rare and endangered species from overexploitation and extinction by concentrating on common and prolific species.

When gathering wild food, foragers also need to take care not to harm or disturb the nearby flora, ecosystems, or wildlife. Plants and fungi that are uprooted, tramped, or otherwise harmed can negatively impact nearby ecosystems, including habitat damage, soil erosion, and biodiversity loss. Consequently, foragers ought to use caution and low-impact harvesting methods, including carefully pulling leaves or fruits from plants, chopping mushrooms off at the base of the stem, and causing the least amount of harm to the nearby flora.

Foragers should not only follow ethical harvesting practices but also take care to leave as little of an ecological imprint as possible on the habitats and ecosystems in which they forage. Foragers ought to refrain from foraging in delicate or protected regions, such as wildlife sanctuaries, nature reserves, and fragile ecosystems like alpine meadows or wetlands. Instead, they ought to concentrate on gathering in more robust ecosystems where their actions are unlikely to result in damage.

In addition, foragers must to be conscious of and mindful of indigenous and cultural knowledge and customs around the gathering of wild foods. Numerous native groups have strong relationships to the land and long-standing customs about resource management and sustainable hunting. Foragers can obtain important insights into sustainable gathering methods and a greater understanding of the significance of maintaining traditional knowledge and cultural legacy by studying from and honoring the wisdom of indigenous peoples. Harvesting in season and moderately is another crucial component of sustainable foraging in order to protect natural populations and maintain the resource's viability. Foragers should refrain from gathering wild foods, for instance, during vulnerable seasons of the year, such as when wildlife is reproducing or when there is environmental hardship or drought. Foragers can lessen their influence on nearby ecosystems and encourage the resilience and natural regeneration of wild populations by harvesting in season and in moderation.

In addition, it is imperative for foragers to adhere to pertinent laws and regulations that control the gathering of wild food in their region. It's important to become informed about the rules and restrictions that many regions have in place to protect cultural resources, endangered animals, and sensitive habitats before participating in any foraging activities. Foragers can ensure that their operations are carried out legally and responsibly and contribute to the protection and sustainable management of wild food resources by adhering to relevant legislation and standards.

Foragers can help conserve and manage wild food supplies in addition to using sustainable foraging methods in the field. They can do this by supporting regional conservation initiatives, taking part in citizen science initiatives, and speaking out in favor of the preservation of biodiversity and natural habitats. Foragers can contribute to the promotion of policies and programs that support the long-term health and resilience of natural ecosystems by collaborating with scientists, conservationists, and policymakers. They can also help to increase awareness about the significance of sustainable foraging habits.

In summary, maintaining the health and resilience of natural ecosystems, as well as safeguarding wild food supplies, needs sustainable foraging techniques. Foragers can reap the benefits of nature's harvest while also helping to ensure the sustainability and care of wild food sources for future generations by harvesting in a way that minimizes adverse effects on the environment, places a high priority on biodiversity conservation, and honors traditional knowledge and cultural heritage. Foragers can play a critical role in promoting the conservation and sustainable management of wild food resources for the benefit of everybody by engaging in responsible harvesting practices, lending support to regional conservation initiatives, and speaking out in favor of preserving natural habitats and biodiversity.

CHAPTER VII

Advanced Topics

Mycorrhizal Relationships in Nature

Earth's terrestrial ecosystems rely heavily on the complex symbiotic partnerships known as mycorrhizal linkages, which occur between fungi and plant roots. The health and proper operation of natural ecosystems depend on these connections because they are critical to the cycling of nutrients, plant development, soil structure, and ecosystem stability. The majority of land plants have their roots colonized by mycorrhizal fungi, which create symbiotic structures called mycorrhizae. These structures allow fungus and plants to exchange nutrients in a mutually advantageous way.

Although many other kinds of mycorrhizal relationships exist, ectomycorrhizae and arbuscular mycorrhizae are the two most prevalent varieties. In order to feed on nutrients like nitrogen, phosphate, and water, ectomycorrhizal fungi create a sheath around the outside of plant roots and expand hyphal networks into the surrounding soil. These mushrooms are frequently found near trees in temperate forests and are essential to the uptake of nutrients and the cycling of carbon in these environments. Conversely, arbuscular mycorrhizal fungi infiltrate plant roots' cells and create complex structures known as vesicles and arbuscules inside the root tissue. These fungi are common in grassland and agricultural environments and play a key role in enhancing plant tolerance to water stress and nutrient uptake.

Mycorrhizal fungi and plants have a symbiotic connection that is based on mutualistic resource exchanges.

Mycorrhizal fungus give plants vital nutrients and water that is taken up from the soil in return for the carbohydrates that the plant produces through photosynthesis. The fungi's vast hyphal network, which can cover a lot more ground than plant roots alone and improves nutrient uptake efficiency and plant growth, facilitates this exchange. Mycorrhizal fungi can also increase soil stability and structure by agglomerating soil particles and increasing soil porosity, which encourages root development and water infiltration.

Beyond just exchanging nutrients, mycorrhizal interactions are essential for plant communication and defense against pests and diseases. According to recent studies, mycorrhizal fungi can serve as go-betweens in underground signaling networks, facilitating communication and information sharing between plants regarding the availability of resources, the state of the environment, and possible dangers. The "wood wide web," an underground network of communication, allows plants to adapt their physiology and behavior to changes in their environment, such as drought, nutrient shortage, or pest invasion.

Furthermore, a process known as "mycorrhiza-induced resistance" allows mycorrhizal fungus to increase a plant's tolerance to pests and diseases. Mycorrhizal fungi help plants resist attacks by infections and herbivores by boosting the plant's immune system and generating antifungal chemicals. This enhances environmental health by lowering the demand for chemical pesticides. Moreover, actinomycetes and bacteria in the soil can work symbiotically with mycorrhizal fungi to enhance soil fertility and plant defense mechanisms.

Mycorrhizal connections are essential for agriculture, forestry, and ecosystem restoration in addition to their ecological significance. Mycorrhizal fungus in agriculture can increase nutrient intake, water stress tolerance, and disease resistance, increasing crop output and resilience. Farmers can boost soil fertility and health, lessen by mycorrhizal inoculants to their agricultural soils, farmers can reduce their dependency on synthetic fertilizers and pesticides and increase crop yields in a sustainable and environmentally responsible manner.

Mycorrhizal fungi are essential to the regeneration of forests and the restoration of ecosystems in forestry. For seedling establishment and growth, many tree species depend on mycorrhizal connections, especially in nutrient-poor soils or disturbed ecosystems. Foresters can increase the durability and success of tree planting operations as well as the ecological functioning of restored ecosystems by learning the mycorrhizal requirements of target tree species and encouraging the development of mycorrhizal fungi in reforestation efforts. Furthermore, the ability of mycorrhizal associations to improve ecosystem resilience and sequester carbon could lessen the effects of climate change. Through the breakdown of plant litter and root exudates, mycorrhizal fungi play a crucial role in the carbon cycle and storage in ecosystems on land. This process transfers carbon from plants to soil organic matter. Mycorrhizal fungi can help lessen the effects of climate change on ecosystems and support international efforts help combat climate change by enhancing soil carbon storage, promoting plant growth, and lowering greenhouse gas emissions.

Mycorrhizal interactions are essential for agriculture and ecology, but they are threatened by pollution, habitat destruction, and climate change, among other human activities. The health and functionality of terrestrial ecosystems can be jeopardized by land degradation, urbanization, agriculture intensification, and deforestation, which can also lower the variety and abundance of mycorrhizal fungi and disrupt mycorrhizal networks. Furthermore, mycorrhizal symbioses can be harmed by pollution from pesticides, fertilizers, and industrial pollutants, This may potentially be harmful to the resilience of ecosystems and plant growth.

In summary, mycorrhizal interactions are vital to terrestrial ecosystems because they support plant growth, soil health, nutrient cycling, and ecosystem resilience. Plants and fungi develop symbiotic partnerships that promote the exchange of nutrients, water, and information. This leads to an increase in plant productivity and defensive mechanisms, as well as the promotion of soil stability and fertility. By understanding and supporting sustainable mycorrhizal techniques in forestry, agriculture, and ecosystem restoration, we may benefit from the ecological advantages of mycorrhizal fungi and guarantee the resilience and health of both natural and managed ecosystems for future generations.

Medicinal Mushrooms: Uses and Benefits

For decades, traditional medical systems worldwide have utilized medicinal mushrooms due to their numerous health advantages and therapeutic qualities. Numerous bioactive substances found in these fungus, such as polysaccharides, antioxidants, triterpenoids, and beta-glucans, contribute to their therapeutic qualities and prospective uses in the treatment of a range of illnesses. Modern research is constantly investigating and studying the myriad possible health benefits that medicinal mushrooms offer, ranging from enhancing the immune system to decreasing inflammation, improving cardiovascular health, and promoting mental well-being.

Ganoderma lucidum, popularly known as reishi or lingzhi, is one of the most well-known medicinal mushrooms. Traditional Chinese medicine has long utilized reishi mushrooms for their immune-modulating, anti-inflammatory, and antioxidant qualities. Reishi mushrooms may be helpful in treating and preventing a variety of illnesses, including allergies, asthma, and autoimmune diseases. Research has indicated that they may also aid improve immune function, lower inflammation, and shield against oxidative stress. Reishi mushrooms have also been investigated for their possible anticancer properties; some studies indicate that they may improve the efficacy of radiation and chemotherapy by preventing tumor development and metastasis.

Commonly referred to as shiitake, Lentinula edodes is another well-liked medicinal fungus. In addition to being highly valued for their meaty texture and rich flavor in cooking, shiitake mushrooms provide many health advantages. Beta-glucans and polysaccharides found in shiitake mushrooms have been demonstrated to enhance immunological function, lower cholesterol, and enhance cardiovascular health. Additionally, research has indicated that shiitake mushrooms may possess antibacterial, anti-inflammatory, and anti-cancer qualities. As such, they are a beneficial supplement to a balanced diet that aims to prevent illness and promote general health.

Several other medicinal mushrooms have drawn interest due to their possible health advantages, in addition to shiitake and reishi. Traditional Chinese medicine values Cordyceps sinensis, a parasitic fungus that develops on caterpillar larvae in the Himalayan region, for its adaptogenic and energy-boosting qualities. Studies have been conducted on cordyceps mushrooms because of their ability to boost respiratory health, increase stamina and endurance, and improve athletic performance. Furthermore, cordyceps mushrooms have the potential to be helpful in the management of diabetes and other chronic diseases since they may lower inflammation, protect against oxidative stress, and help regulate blood sugar levels.

In addition, there has been interest in Hericium erinaceus, popularly known as lion's mane, due to its possible neuroprotective and cognitive-enhancing properties. Hericenones and erinacines, two substances found in lion's mane mushrooms, have been demonstrated to increase the synthesis of nerve growth factor (NGF) and encourage the development and regeneration of brain nerve cells. According to studies, lion's mane mushrooms may help prevent age-related cognitive decline and neurodegenerative illnesses like Alzheimer's and Parkinson's, as well as boost memory and learning. Lion's mane mushrooms are a promising natural treatment for mental health and wellbeing since they have also been investigated for possible antidepressant and anxiolytic properties.

Furthermore, South Americans have long utilized Agaricus blazei, commonly referred to as the Brazilian mushroom or Himematsutake, for its anti-cancer and immune-stimulating abilities. Beta-glucans, polysaccharides, and other bioactive substances found in Agaricus blazei mushrooms have been demonstrated to improve immune function, promote the generation of immune cells, and impede the growth and metastasis of tumors. Research findings indicate that Agaricus blazei mushrooms may hold promise for the prevention and treatment of cancer, in addition to their potential benefits in managing other chronic illnesses such as high blood pressure, diabetes, and high cholesterol.

Furthermore, a number of additional medicinal mushrooms have been investigated for their possible therapeutic and health benefits, such as Phellinus linteus (Sanghuang), Grifola frondosa (Maitake), and Trametes versicolor (Turkey tail). These mushrooms are rich in bioactive chemicals that have anti-inflammatory, anti-cancer, immune-modulating, and antioxidant properties, making them a fantastic complement to a healthy diet and way of life. Preliminary studies and anecdotal data indicate that these mushrooms may offer a range of health advantages for increasing general well-being and lifespan. However, further research is necessary to fully understand the mechanisms of action and therapeutic potential of these mushrooms.

In summary, medicinal mushrooms are a great complement to a balanced diet and way of life because they have a wide range of possible health advantages and therapeutic qualities. Medicinal mushrooms have long been valued for their therapeutic qualities. They can reduce inflammation, strengthen the immune system, promote cardiovascular health, improve mental health, and guard against chronic illnesses, including cancer and neurological diseases. As scientific investigations into the mechanisms of action and therapeutic potential of these fungi proceed, they are becoming more widely acknowledged as beneficial natural therapies for enhancing longevity and health in the contemporary world. Medicinal mushrooms can be a tasty and practical method to support your general health and well-being for years to come, whether they are eaten fresh, dried, or as supplements.

Mycoremediation: Fungi's Role in Environmental Cleanup

Mycoremediation, the process of using fungus to break down, sequester, or change environmental toxins, has become a viable and long-term method of cleaning the environment. Because of their special metabolic routes and enzymatic properties, fungi can degrade a variety of organic and inorganic pollutants, such as pesticides, heavy metals, petroleum hydrocarbons, and even radioactive isotopes. Mycoremediation is a low-cost, environmentally acceptable, and non-invasive substitute for conventional remediation techniques like chemical treatment or excavation by utilizing the inherent capabilities of fungi.

The use of oyster mushrooms (Pleurotus ostreatus) to break down hydrocarbon pollutants in contaminated soil and water is one of the most well-known applications of mycoremediation. Polycyclic aromatic hydrocarbons (PAHs), a prevalent contaminant found in soil and water close to industrial sites, landfills, and oil spills, are broken down extremely well by oyster mushrooms. According to studies, PAHs can be detoxified and metabolized by oyster mushrooms using enzymatic processes. This process transforms the PAHs into less toxic, simpler molecules that can either be integrated into the fungal biomass or released back into the environment in a less dangerous form.

Comparably, the capacity of white-rot fungi, like those in the genera Phanerochaete and Trametes, to break down lignin—a complex polymer present in wood and plant debris—as well as a variety of resistant pollutants, such as dioxins, PCBs, and chlorinated solvents, has been the subject of extensive research. An extensive variety of lignin-degrading enzymes, including laccase, manganese peroxidase, and lignin peroxidase, are produced by white-rot fungus. These enzymes allow the lignin and other complex organic compounds to be broken down into simpler molecules that can be mineralized or taken up by other microbes. When stubborn contaminants endanger human health and the environment, contaminated soils, sediments, and wastewater can be remedied via this method called ligninolysis.

Furthermore, by promoting plant growth and nutrient uptake in damaged or contaminated settings, mycorrhizal fungi—which develop symbiotic relationships with the roots of most land plants—play a critical role in soil remediation and ecosystem restoration. By immobilizing heavy metals and other hazardous molecules like arsenic, cadmium, and lead in the soil, securing them in fungal tissues, or changing them into less harmful forms, mycorrhizal fungi can aid plants in withstanding and detoxifying these substances. Mycorrhizal fungi can also increase soil aggregation and water retention, improve soil structure and fertility, and encourage the development of native flora in contaminated or disturbed habitats, all of which contribute to the resilience and function of ecosystems.

Moreover, some fungal species—referred to as hyperaccumulators—have the unique capacity to concentrate and accumulate high concentrations of heavy metals in their tissues without experiencing harmful side effects. Through a process known as bioaccumulation or phytoremediation, these metal-accumulating fungi, which include those in the genus Aspergillus, Penicillium, and Trichoderma, can be utilized to extract metals from contaminated soils, sediments, and industrial wastes. After the metal-contaminated biomass has been gathered, it can be appropriately disposed of or processed further to extract valuable metals for recycling or other uses. This eliminates the need for traditional mining and metal extraction techniques, which can have detrimental effects on the environment.

Fungi are essential to bioremediation because they not only have the capacity to break down organic contaminants and sequester heavy metals, but they also increase soil microbial diversity and activity, stimulate soil carbon sequestration, and aid in the breakdown and decomposition of organic matter. In order to break down complex organic compounds like cellulose, hemicellulose, and lignin into simpler molecules that can be assimilated by other microorganisms or incorporated into soil organic matter, fungi produce a variety of extracellular enzymes, including cellulases, hemicellulases, and ligninases. By assisting in the cycling of carbon and nutrients through the soil food web, this process—known as saprotrophic decomposition—improves soil productivity and fertility while lowering the accumulation of organic pollutants and toxins.

Additionally, fungi can be extremely important in the bioremediation of damaged water bodies, such as wetlands, lakes, and rivers, where industrial chemicals, pesticides, and medicines are among the pollutants that endanger human health and aquatic ecosystems. Pesticides, herbicides, medicines, and industrial chemicals are just a few of the organic pollutants that can be broken down and detoxified by fungi via enzymatic reactions and metabolic pathways that change these substances into less harmful, simpler forms. Fungi can also aid in the removal of surplus nutrients from water bodies, such as phosphorus and nitrogen, lowering the danger of eutrophication and algal blooms, which reduce oxygen levels and endanger aquatic life.

Furthermore, where contaminants like formaldehyde, mold spores, and volatile organic compounds (VOCs) endanger human health and indoor air quality, fungi can be quite helpful in cleaning up contaminated air and indoor spaces. It has been demonstrated that several fungal species, including Aspergillus, Penicillium, and Trichoderma, may break down and detoxify volatile organic compounds (VOCs) and other indoor air pollutants by breaking them down into simpler, less hazardous molecules through enzymatic reactions and metabolic pathways. Additionally, by competing with mold spores for resources and space, preventing their germination and proliferation, and fostering a healthy indoor microbiome, fungi can help regulate indoor mold growth and lower the risk of mold-related health issues.

To sum up, mycoremediation uses the innate ability of fungus to break down, absorb, and change a variety of organic and inorganic contaminants, providing a viable and long-term method of environmental cleanup. Fungi play a vital part in remediation and restoration efforts globally, from breaking down hydrocarbon pollutants in soil and water to sequestering heavy metals, improving soil fertility, and fostering ecosystem resilience. We can manage environmental contamination and pollution in a non-invasive, environmentally friendly, and cost-effective way by using fungi, protecting the ecosystem and human health for future generations.

Fungal Diversity and Conservation

Among the most varied and ecologically significant types of organisms on Earth are fungi, which are essential to the cycling of nutrients, decomposition, symbiotic relationships, and the health of ecosystems. Fungi show an incredible diversity of forms, lives, and ecological tactics, ranging from microscopic single-celled yeasts to enormous, multicellular mushrooms and molds, with an estimated 2.2 to 3.8 million species worldwide. In comparison to other categories of species, like plants and animals, fungal diversity is still vastly understudied and poorly understood, which presents serious obstacles to conservation efforts and the sustainable management of fungal biodiversity.

A vast variety of biological niches and habitats, including both terrestrial and aquatic settings, woods, grasslands, deserts, and even extreme settings like deep-sea vents, arctic regions, and hot springs, are included in the category of fungal diversity. Almost every ecosystem on Earth has fungi, which are essential to the decomposition of organic matter, nutrient cycling, soil formation, and interactions between plants and microbes. Fungi function as decomposers, reducing complex organic materials like cellulose, lignin, and chitin to simpler molecules that other creatures may recycle and utilize again, thus enhancing the general well-being and productivity of ecosystems.

Furthermore, a variety of plants, animals, and microbes have symbiotic relationships with fungus, such as mycorrhizal fungi, lichens, endophytes, and gut fungi, which offer vital functions and advantages to their hosts. For instance, most terrestrial plants' roots create symbiotic relationships with mycorrhizal fungi, which promote plant growth, nutrient uptake, and stress tolerance by allowing the movement of nutrients between fungi and plants. In terrestrial ecosystems, lichens— symbiotic relationships between fungi and algae or cyanobacteria—are crucial for soil stabilization, nitrogen fixation, and carbon sequestration.

Fungal diversity is essential to the environment, but human activity threatens it in many ways. These include habitat destruction, pollution, climate change, invasive species, and overuse of natural resources. Fungal biodiversity is seriously threatened by habitat loss and fragmentation brought on by deforestation, urbanization, agriculture, and infrastructure development. This results in the loss of vital habitats and ecosystems where fungi are essential to the cycling of nutrients, the formation of soil, and the operation of ecosystems. In addition to damaging fungal populations, pollution from industrial and agricultural sources can also change the chemistry of soil, interfere with microbial interactions, and weaken the resilience and health of ecosystems.

In addition, global changes in temperature and precipitation patterns, disruption of seasonal cycles, and reorganization of species' ranges and habitats are all consequences of climate change that affect fungal diversity and distribution patterns. The growth and reproduction of fungi, the composition and structure of fungal communities, and the frequency and severity of fungal illnesses and infections in plants, animals, and humans can all be impacted by variations in temperature and precipitation. Furthermore, invasive species can outcompete native fungus, disturb ecological processes, endanger native biodiversity, and undermine the stability of ecosystems. Examples of such invasive species include exotic fungi brought in by international trade and tourism.

Numerous obstacles stand in the way of conservation initiatives meant to preserve fungal diversity and ecosystems, such as a lack of taxonomic understanding, low public awareness, and insufficient financing and resources for both study and conservation. Despite playing vital ecological roles and having the potential to be economically and medicinally significant, fungi are frequently disregarded and understudied in comparison to plants and animals. Accurately identifying and categorizing fungal species, evaluating their conservation status, and allocating conservation efforts to species and ecosystems most in danger all depend on taxonomic expertise.

Furthermore, in order to promote conservation efforts, raise awareness of the importance of fungal diversity, and foster stewardship of fungal habitats and biodiversity, public education and awareness campaigns are crucial. The public can be involved in fungal conservation and study, encouraged to participate in data collection and monitoring activities, and encouraged to recognize the ecological, cultural, and economic significance of fungus through outreach initiatives, citizen science projects, and educational initiatives.

Moreover, more financing and resources are required to support studies, observations, and conservation initiatives pertaining to the biodiversity and habitats of fungi. The understanding of fungal diversity and ecology may be improved, information gaps can be filled, and evidence-based conservation policies and management practices can be informed by investments in taxonomy research, molecular genetics, ecological monitoring, and habitat restoration. To effectively create and implement conservation strategies and regulations that protect fungal variety and ecosystems for future generations, scientists, policymakers, conservation organizations, indigenous people, and local stakeholders must collaborate.

In summary, fungal diversity is an important part of the world's biodiversity since it is vital to the functioning of ecosystems, the cycling of nutrients, and ecological processes all over the planet. Fungi are important to the environment, but they also face a number of dangers, including as habitat loss, pollution, climate change, invasive species, and overuse of natural resources. For this reason, it is important to boost conservation efforts and manage fungal biodiversity sustainably. Through promoting stewardship, raising awareness, and providing funds for conservation and research initiatives, we can help safeguard and preserve fungal diversity and ecosystems for the benefit of present and future generations.

CHAPTER VIII

Troubleshooting and FAQs

Dealing with Pests and Diseases

An unavoidable obstacle for farmers in any agricultural activity, including mushroom growing, is dealing with pests and illnesses. Despite their reputation for adaptation and resistance, pests and viruses can still represent a threat to mushrooms. If left unchecked, these challenges can impede growth, lower yields, or even result in crop failure. For mushroom cultivation to be successful, it is therefore crucial to comprehend the frequent pests and diseases that affect the crops and to put efficient management techniques into place.

For mushroom growers, pests are a significant worry since they can quickly infest and damage mushroom beds, resulting in large production losses. The mushroom fly, or Drosophila spp., is one of the most infamous pests in mushroom farming. These small flies are attracted to decomposing organic waste, like a mushroom substrate, and lay their eggs in the moist environment of the growing medium. The fruiting bodies and mycelium are what the larvae of mushroom flies consume after hatching, resulting in significant pollution and destruction. Strict sanitation procedures are necessary to prevent mushroom fly infestations. These procedures include prompt removal of spent mushroom blocks, appropriate composting of substrate materials, and routine washing and disinfection of growth facilities

The Tyrophagus spp. Mushroom mite, which feeds on mycelium and mushroom tissue and causes stunted growth, distortion, and discoloration of fruiting bodies, is another frequent pest faced by mushroom farmers. If left unchecked, these tiny pests can swiftly proliferate and spread throughout mushroom crops, preferring warm, humid settings. Maintaining ideal environmental conditions, such as appropriate ventilation, humidity control, and temperature management, together with the use of biological control techniques, like predatory mites or nematodes, to decrease mite populations, are essential to preventing mushroom mite infestations.

In addition to pests, a range of bacterial, viral, and fungal diseases can infect and quickly spread throughout entire cultures if they are not controlled. Green mold, a fungal disease produced by species of Trichoderma, is one of the most common problems that mushroom growers deal with. This opportunistic fungus can swiftly dominate mushroom beds and growing substrates, competing with mycelium for nutrients and space. It grows best in warm, humid environments. If green mold infections are not treated immediately, they may lead to low-quality fruiting bodies, lower yields, and crop loss. Growers need to follow stringent hygiene and sanitation protocols, which include routinely washing and disinfecting growing rooms, tools, and equipment to avoid green mold infections.

For mushroom farmers, bacterial illnesses can also present serious difficulties. These diseases can cause symptoms including soft rot, bacterial blotch, and bacterial spot, which can result in fruiting body deformation, discoloration, and decay. These illnesses can spread quickly in warm, humid situations and are frequently brought into mushroom-growing habitats by contaminated substrate, water, or equipment. Strict biosecurity protocols, such as the isolation of fresh mushroom cultures, cleaning of instruments and equipment, and the use of disease-resistant strains of mushrooms, are necessary to prevent bacterial infections.

Moreover, viral infections can harm mushroom farms, resulting in symptoms like crop loss and decreased yields along with yellowing, stunting, and deformation of fruiting bodies. If left unchecked, viral infections can spread quickly within and between mushroom cultures. They are typically transferred by contaminated substrate, diseased mushroom cultures, or vector species like insects or mites. Growers need to take strong biosecurity precautions, such as quarantining new mushroom cultures, cleaning tools and equipment, and using virus- free planting material, to prevent viral infections.

Preventive measures are frequently the most effective when it comes to controlling pests and illnesses in mushroom farming. Growers can lower the danger of diseases and pests and lessen the need for chemical interventions by using stringent sanitation procedures, preserving ideal environmental conditions, and employing effective crop management measures. When illnesses and pests do, however, manifest themselves, it is crucial to act quickly to limit losses and stop additional harm. This could include applying biological control agents, like nematodes or predatory insects, cultural control techniques, such as crop rotation or sterilizing growing substrates, or, as a last resort, chemical treatments, like fungicides or bactericides.

In conclusion, managing diseases and pests is a constant struggle for mushroom farmers that call for awareness, expertise, and preventative measures. Growers may reduce the risk of infestations and infections, and maintain the health and productivity of their mushroom cultures by being aware of the typical pests and diseases that affect mushroom crops and putting appropriate preventative and management measures in place. A healthy and resilient mushroom crop in the face of changing pests and disease challenges depend on continuous research and development of novel control techniques, such as biological control agents, genetic resistance, and integrated pest management strategies.

Common Questions Answered

A gratifying and fascinating hobby, mushroom farming draws fans from all walks of life. But it's also a complex procedure with lots of subtleties and complexity that might be confusing for newcomers. For those starting out in mushroom production, there are many questions to answer, ranging from selecting the ideal substrate to controlling pests and diseases. This section will address some of the most frequent queries posed by would-be mushroom growers and offer thorough responses to assist them in navigating the fungal world.

"What substrate should I use?" is one of the first queries that novices frequently have. Growing media, also known as the substrate, is an essential part of mushroom culture because it supplies the nutrients and support needed for the formation of fruiting bodies and mycelium growth. The choice of substrate is contingent upon the type of mushroom being farmed, availability, and climatic conditions like temperature and humidity. Among the many alternatives are straw, sawdust, and compost. For instance, shiitake mushrooms (Lentinula edodes) like hardwood sawdust or logs, whereas oyster mushrooms (Pleurotus spp.) are typically grown on pasteurized straw or enriched sawdust. It is crucial to investigate the particular needs of the mushroom species you plan to expand and select a substrate that satisfies those needs.

"How do I inoculate my substrate?" is another frequently asked question. The process of inoculating a substrate with mycelium culture, or mushroom spawn, to start the colonization and growth phase. Grain spawn, liquid culture, and agar wedges are a few of the inoculation techniques; each has benefits and drawbacks. For instance, grain spawn—sterilized grains that have been colonized by mycelium—is frequently utilized to inoculate large surfaces like sawdust or straw. However, mycelium is suspended in a nutrient-rich liquid media in liquid culture, which can be employed to make grain spawn or inoculate smaller surfaces. Agar wedges, which are tiny mycelium fragments cultivated on nutrient agar plates, can be utilized to produce grain spawn or directly inoculate substrates. The size of the cultivation, the desired rate of colonization, and the availability of resources are some of the criteria that influence the choice of inoculation technique.

During the cultivation phase, "How do I maintain optimal environmental conditions?" is a common question. Environmental elements that might affect a mushroom's growth and development include temperature, humidity, light, and air quality. Mushrooms are extremely sensitive to these elements. For instance, shiitake mushrooms prefer colder temperatures and higher humidity levels, but oyster mushrooms grow best in warm, humid environments with sufficient air exchange. To guarantee ideal growth and fruiting, it is crucial to continuously monitor and regulate the environmental conditions during the growing process. This may entail creating the right lighting conditions for fruiting bodies to form, as well as controlling temperature and humidity levels via heaters, humidifiers, fans, and other equipment.

"How do I prevent pests and diseases?" is one of mushroom producers' most frequent concerns. If left unchecked, pests and illnesses can wreak havoc on mushroom fields, leading to lower yields, lower-quality fruiting bodies, and possibly crop loss. Growers should follow stringent sanitation and hygiene practices, such as routinely washing and sanitizing tools, equipment, and growing sites, to avoid pest and disease issues. Furthermore, biological control agents and vent screening are examples of preventive methods that can be used to keep diseases and pests at bay. In the event that insect or disease issues arise, it is crucial to identify and treat them as soon as possible to limit losses and stop more harm.

The question "When and how do I harvest my mushrooms?" is another that is frequently asked. Since harvesting affects both the crop's quality and productivity, it is an essential stage in the mushroom farming process. The type of mushroom being grown, along with the time at which the fruiting bodies are developing, determine when and how to harvest. For instance, shiitake mushrooms are usually picked when the caps are still securely closed. Still, oyster mushrooms are generally harvested when the caps are fully opened but before the veil breaks. In order to prevent mycelium damage and the dissemination of spores, which can cause contamination and disease, mushroom harvesting must be done correctly.

And last, one of the most frequent queries from novices is, "What should I do with my harvested mushrooms?" Mushrooms can be eaten raw or dry or processed to make various goods like extracts, powders, and supplements. In addition to being prepared in many different ways, such as soups, stir-fries, salads, and pasta dishes, fresh mushrooms can be frozen or dried and kept for later use. While supplements and extracts made from dried mushrooms are frequently utilized for their therapeutic and health advantages, dried mushrooms can also be rehydrated and used in cooking. Mushrooms may be used in countless ways for both culinary and medicinal purposes, which makes them an invaluable and adaptable addition to any kitchen or medicine cabinet.
In conclusion, growing mushrooms is an enlightening and fulfilling pastime that presents countless chances for research and discovery. Beginners can acquire the information and self-assurance they need to effectively

produce their mushrooms at home by answering frequently asked questions and concerns. In the world of fungi, there's always something new to learn, regardless of how long you've been growing mushrooms.

CONCLUSION

Finally, for anyone who is fascinated by the complex world of fungus, "The Mycophile's Handbook: From Spores to Harvest: Your Comprehensive Guide to Mushroom" is a vital resource. This handbook provides readers with all the information and abilities they need to effectively cultivate mushrooms at home or on a larger scale, starting with the basic steps of spore selection and ending with the ultimate harvest.

Its thorough treatment of mushroom biology, growth methods, and valuable tips guarantees that readers of all skill levels—from beginners to seasoned growers—can profit from its insights. The book explores the culinary and medical uses of mushrooms, inspiring readers to include them in regular meals and drawing attention to their potential therapeutic and health advantages.

Furthermore, "The Mycophile's Handbook" promotes a greater understanding of the ecological importance of mushrooms as well as their part in environmentally responsible farming practices. The book vividly captures the richness and beauty of mushrooms with its easily understood language, concise explanations, and striking graphics, piquing readers' interest and igniting their desire to learn more.

"The Mycophile's Handbook" is really a portal to a greater comprehension of the natural world and our connectivity with it rather than merely a guide to mushroom production. This handbook is a reliable guide for anyone venturing into the fascinating world of mushrooms, be they new to the process or looking to brush up on their knowledge and abilities.

In conclusion, "My Mycophile's Handbook" seeks to illuminate the captivating world of fungi, serving as a gateway for enthusiasts to delve into the depths of mycology. Through its pages, we've explored the diversity, ecology, and cultural significance of fungi, unraveling their mysteries and highlighting their vital roles in the ecosystem and human life. May this handbook inspire curiosity, foster understanding, and spark a lifelong passion for mycology among its readers. As we continue to explore and appreciate the fungal kingdom, let us remember to tread lightly, with respect for the delicate balance of nature, and embrace the wonder that fungi offer to those willing to observe and learn.

Thank you for buying and reading/ listening to our book.

If you found this book useful or helpful, please take a few minutes and leave a review on the platform where you purchased our book.

Your feedback matters greatly to us.

www.ingramcontent.com/pod-product-compliance
Lightning Source LLC
Chambersburg PA
CBHW052043150726

48002CB00002B/727